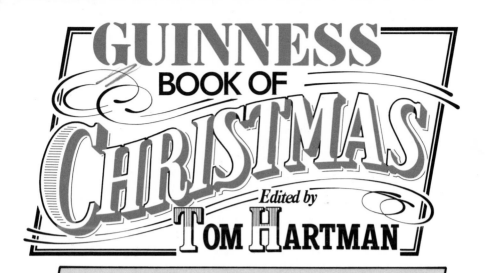

GUINNESS BOOK OF CHRISTMAS

Edited by

TOM HARTMAN

WITH *CARTOONS BY*
WONK AND
PETER HARRIS

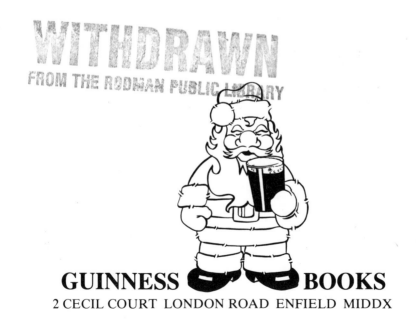

GUINNESS BOOKS

2 CECIL COURT LONDON ROAD ENFIELD MIDDX

394.268
G964
A-1

The editor and publishers wish to thank and acknowledge Nigel Fitt of the Post Office for his assistance.
Acknowledgment is also made to *The Times* newspaper for permission to reproduce the article on page 32 by Robin Young.
The recipes on pages 71, 76 and 81 come from *Cooking for Christmas* by Josceline Dimbleby, published for J. Sainsbury plc and available from their stores. Recipes © Josceline Dimbleby 1978.
Picture Acknowledgements: All Sport 131, 135; N S Barrett 126; BBC Hulton Picture Library 37 (left), 39, 138, 141, 142, 143, 144; Mary Evans Picture Library 34, 61, 63; Field Communications 70; Mansell Collection 9, 13, 25 (bottom), 71, 82; Pictorial Press Ltd 19, 43, 44, 45, 47, 51; The Post Office 83, 87, 93, 96, 99, 101, 102, 103, 108; Fred Specovius 105, 106; Syndication International 18 (bottom)

Editor: Alex E Reid; Design and Layout: David Roberts; Cover Design: David Roberts; Artwork: Peter Harris and Brian Robins; Picture Research: Sheila Goldsmith; Additional Artwork: Eddie Botchway; Cartoons by Wonk

© **Tom Hartman and Guinness Superlatives Ltd 1984**

Published in Great Britain by
Guinness Superlatives Ltd, 2 Cecil Court,
London Road, Enfield, Middlesex EN2 6DJ
Distributed in the USA by Sterling Publishing Co Inc,
2 Park Avenue, New York.

'Guinness' is a registered trade mark of
Guinness Superlatives Ltd

British Library Cataloguing in Publication Data

The Guinness book of Christmas.
1. Christmas
I. Hartman, Tom
394.2′68282   GT4985
ISBN 0-85112-404-6

38212001287785
Main Adult
394.268 G964
Guinness book of Christmas

Typeset, printed and bound in Great Britain by
Hazell Watson & Viney Limited,
Member of the BPCC Group,
Aylesbury, Bucks

Contents

3

I n these pages the great festival of Christmas is looked at in the Guinness style. The *Guinness Book of Records* has, since the first edition was published some 30 years ago, become an international bestseller and is recognised world-wide as the authority on superlative achievements. From this base Guinness Books has developed a wide range of titles, exploring the superlatives of particular subjects and it is the authors of these books who have contributed to this, the *Guinness Book of Christmas.*

Patrick Moore, author of *The Guinness Book of Astronomy Facts and Feats*, looks at the Christmas sky; James Mackay, author of *The Guinness Book of Stamps Facts and Feats* discusses Christmas stamps, coins and places with a Christmas flavour; the husband and wife team of Robert and Celia Dearling, who have written *The Guinness Book of Music* and *The Guinness Book of Recorded Sound*, talk about Christmas carols and other Christmas music: Ingrid Holford, author of *The Guinness Book of Weather Facts and Feats*, looks at white Christmases and weather conditions in general at this time of year. The second bestseller in the Guinness range is *The Guinness Book of British Hit Singles* and its compilers, the brothers Tim and Jo Rice, Paul Gambaccini and Mike Read list and discuss the Christmas hits. The work of these authors and many more from the Guinness stable is co-ordinated by the editor, Tom Hartman, author of *The Guinness Book of Ships and Shipping.*

Guinness present this book as a treasure trove of fascinating information about Christmas and Christmasy events. We hope that we have, again, captured the Guinness style for authoritative information. Such material can be regarded as useful or useless according to taste, but we hope that Guinness readers will enjoy it and, of course, have a very happy Christmas.

Peter Matthews: *Editorial Director, Guinness Books Ltd*

I

Origins and Decorations

The Origins of Christmas

Everyone knows that Christmas Day falls on 25 December and that it is the day on which we celebrate the birth of Jesus Christ. But, as there can be no shadow of doubt that Jesus Christ was *not*, in fact, born on 25 December, AD 1, how did it come about that we celebrate His birthday on that particular day and that this year we will be calling it Christmas, *1984*?

Let us examine the second question first. We owe our method of numbering the years to a Russian monk called Dionysius Exiguus ('the little') who moved to Italy and in AD 533 first started to reckon dates from the birth of Christ. Hitherto the years had been dated from the foundation of Rome which corresponds in the Dionysian calendar to 753 BC. Dates so expressed were preceded by the letters AUC, standing either for *Ab Urbe Condita* (from the foundation of the city) or for *Anno Urbis Conditae* (in the year of the founding of the city). But since we know from St Matthew that Jesus Christ was born in Bethlehem of Judea, in the days of Herod the King, and we also know that Herod died in March of the year AUC 750, it is at once clear that Dionysius was *at least* 3 years out. Theologians, historians, astronomers and a variety of other experts continue to argue the toss about the most probable year of the birth of Our Lord, but, apart from saying that it can not have been after 3 BC, one can only add that, for a variety of reasons, recent scholarship now seems to be generally in favour of the

Dionysius was at least 3 years out

year 8 BC (*pace* astronomer Patrick Moore
– see p. 64).

Let us now consider how the 25th of
December came to be chosen as the day on
which we celebrate the birth of Jesus Christ.
In the early Christian era Mithraism, a
Persian cult which, according to Plutarch,
was introduced to Rome by Pompey's pir-
ate captives from Cilicia in 68 BC, appeared
for a time to be a serious rival to Christianity, to which indeed it bore many simi-
larities, not least in its monotheistic
tendencies, its sacraments, its comparatively high morality, its doctrine of an
Intercessor and a Redeemer and its belief
in a future life and a judgment to come.
Moreover, Sunday was its holy day, dedicated to the worship of the sun. It also
enjoyed the great advantage of being the
fashionable faith of the Roman army.
Gradually, however, Mithraism was driven
out by Christianity, but not without the
latter borrowing quite freely from the for-
mer. To jump ahead a bit in time, we find
St Gregory (Pope Gregory I) writing to St
Augustine, the first Archbishop of Canterbury, in about AD 600 regarding the
best means of converting the Anglo-
Saxons to Christianity and advising
him to accommodate the
ceremonies of the
Christian Church as
much as possible to
those of the heathen.

St Gregory writes to St Augustine

In pagan Rome the Mithraic festival of the Winter Solstice, the *Dies Natalis Solis Invicti* or Day of the Birth of the Unconquered Sun, fell in the middle of the feast of *Saturnalia*, on what corresponds to 25 December in our calendar. Though various scholars have put forward many other ingenious theories to explain why we celebrate Christmas on 25 December, it seems reasonable to assume that the advice St Gregory gave to St Augustine was already being put into practice in the latter part of the fourth century, when the date of Christmas became established, and that the birthday of Our Lord simply replaced the birthday of the sun.

But when exactly *did* the date of Christmas become established? Once again it is impossible to say. The first mention of a Nativity feast on 25 December occurs in a Roman text known as the Philocalian Calendar, because the title page bears the inscription '*Furius Dionysius Philocalus titulavit*', or sometimes as the Liberian Catalogue, because it contains, among other things, a list of the Roman Bishops, or Popes, from St Peter to Liberius (352–66). The Philocalian Calendar dates from the year 354 but is known to embody an older document dating back to 336 and it is not certain whether the reference to the feast of the Nativity belongs to the earlier or the later part. Most scholars favour the later date, so it can be said that, in Rome at least, Christmas was being celebrated on 25 December by 354 at the latest.

In the Eastern Church – in Constantinople, Antioch and Alexandria – the feast of the Epiphany, celebrated on 6 January, marked both the Nativity and the Baptism of Our Lord, but by the middle of the fifth century most of the East had separated the two festivals and adopted 25 December as the feast of the Nativity. The Church of Jerusalem, however, stuck to 6 January until 549 and to this day the Armenian Church celebrates Christmas Day on 6 January.

For us, however, and however incorrectly, the date of the Nativity has been fixed until 'the dust return to the earth as it was; and the spirit return unto God who gave it'.

TH

An Ode on the Birth of our Saviour

Robert Herrick

In Numbers and but these few,
I sing Thy Birth, Oh JESU!
Thou prettie Babie, borne here,
With sup'rabundant scorn here:
Who for Thy Princely Port here,
　　Hadst for Thy place
　　Of Birth, a base
Out-stable for thy Court here.

　　　　Instead of neat Inclosures
　　　　Of inter-woven Osiers;
　　　　Instead of fragrant Posies
　　　　Of Daffadills, and Roses;
　　　　Thy cradle, Kingly Stranger,
　　　　　　As Gospell tells,
　　　　　　Was nothing els,
　　　　But, here, a homely manger.

But we with Silks, (not Cruells)
With sundry precious Jewells,
And Lilly-work will dresse Thee;
And as we dispossesse thee
Of clouts, wee'l make a chamber,
　　　Sweet Babe, for Thee,
　　　Of Ivorie,
And plaister'd round with Amber.

　　　　The Jewes they did disdaine Thee,
　　　　But we will entertaine Thee
　　　　With Glories to await here
　　　　Upon Thy Princely State here,
　　　　And more for love, then pittie.
　　　　　　From yeere to yeere
　　　　　　Wee'l make Thee, here,
　　　　A Free-born of our Citie.

The Oxen Pay Homage to the Christ Child

A superstitious notion prevails in West Devonshire that, at twelve o'clock at night on Christmas Eve, the oxen in their stalls are always found on their knees, as in an attitude of devotion; and that (which is still more singular) since the alteration of the style they continue to do this only on the Eve of old Christmas Day.* An honest countryman, living on the edge of St Stephen's Down, near Launceston, Cornwall, informed me, October 28th, 1790, that he once, with some others, made a trial of the truth of the above, and watching several oxen in their stalls at the above time, at twelve o'clock at night, they observed the two oldest oxen only fall upon their knees, and, as he expressed it in the idiom of the country, make 'a cruel moan like Christian creatures.' I could not but with great difficulty keep my countenance: he saw, and seemed angry that I gave so little credit to his tale, and, walking off in a pettish humour, seemed to 'marvel at my unbelief'. There is an old print of the Nativity, in which the oxen in the stable, near the Virgin and Child, are represented upon their knees, as in a suppliant posture. This graphic representation has probably given rise to the above superstitious notion in his head.

'I could not but with great difficulty keep my countenance'

John Brand Popular Antiquities of Great Britain *1870*

* England switched from the Old Style (Julian) calendar to the new Style (Gregorian) by Act of Parliament in March 1751. This enacted that Wednesday 2 September 1752 should be followed by Thursday 14 September.

he oxen were used in those days for working in the fields; every one had a name, which was called as each was toasted. This night, say the old folks, was the 'real Christmas'. 'My grandfather always kept up Christmas on old Christmas day,' said W—— P——, of Peterchurch, 'none of your new Christmas for him; it must be the real Christmas, too, for the Holy Thorn blossoms, and the cattle go down on their knees at twelve o'clock in remembrance.' I have talked to many people who firmly believed this; though they have not seen it, their parents or grandparents have. Mrs H——, of Eardisley, said that her father, who used to live at Peterchurch, had seen it, and the cattle did not only kneel down, but the tears ran down their cheeks. In Weobley they say that it is only three-year-old oxen that kneel, not those only two years old; but at Kingstone the Vicar was told that it was done only by the seven-year-old oxen, the same age as those in the stable at Bethlehem when Christ was born.

E M Leather The Folk-Lore of Herefordshire *1912*

The Nativity

The thatch on the roof was as golden
Though dusty the straw was and old,
The wind had a peal as of trumpets,
Though blowing and barren and cold,
The mother's hair was a glory
Though loosened and torn,
For under the eaves in the gloaming
    A child was born.

Have a myriad children been quickened,
Have a myriad children grown old,
Grown gross and unloved and embittered,
Grown cunning and savage and cold?
God abides in a terrible patience,
Unangered, unworn,
And again for the child that was squandered
      A child is born.

What know we of aeons behind us,
Dim dynasties lost long ago,
Huge empires, like dreams unremembered,
Huge cities for ages laid low?
This at least – that with blight and with blessing,
With flower and with thorn,
Love was there, and his cry was among them,
      'A child is born.'

Though the darkness be noisy with systems,
Dark fancies that fret and disprove,
Still the plumes stir around us, above us
The wings of the shadow of love:
Oh! princes and priests, have ye seen it
Grow pale through your scorn;
Huge dawns sleep before us, deep changes,
      A child is born.

And the rafters of toil still are gilded
With the dawn of the stars of the heart,
And the wise men draw near in the twilight,
Who are weary of learning and art,
And the face of the tyrant is darkened,
His spirit is torn,
For a new king is enthroned; yea, the sternest,
      A child is born.

And the mother still joys for the whispered
First stir of unspeakable things,
Still feels that high moment unfurling
Red glory of Gabriel's wings.
Still the babe of an hour is a master
Whom angels adorn,
Emmanuel, prophet, anointed,
      A child is born.

And thou, that art still in thy cradle,
The sun being crown for thy brow,
Make answer, our flesh, make an answer,
Say, whence art thou come – who art thou?
Art thou come back on earth for our teaching
To train or to warn –?
Hush – how may we know? – knowing only
A child is born.

G K Chesterton

Some 'Christmas' Words

Christmas

The 'mas' in Christmas has the same derivation as the Mass or eucharistic service of the Roman Catholic Church in the West. The name originated from the words *Ite, Missa Est* (**Go, it is** ended) with which the rite concluded, the word *missa* coming to mean dismissal and finally becoming the name of the rite itself. The earliest known example of the word belongs to the last quarter of the fourth century, occurring in the *Epistles of St Ambrose* and the *Itinerary of Silvia of Aquitania*. Though used in the general sense of 'religious service', in an eminent sense it always denoted the Eucharist. The suffix also survives in Michaelmas, Lammas and Candlemas.

Yule

The derivation of the word is obscure, the most likely source being an old Norse word *jol*, a heathen feast lasting twelve days. In Anglo-Saxon the month of December was known as *aerre-geola* (before Yule) and January as *aftera-geola* (after Yule). Since at least AD 900 Yuletide has been synonymous with Christmas time.

Nowel An expression of joy originally to commemorate the birth of Christ. From the Latin *natalis*, via the French noel. 'One of the peculiarities of Gaulish Latin was a tendency to drop a "t" when that consonant came between two unstressed vowels, and to replace the "t" by a sort of abrupt pause, known to grammarians as "the glottal stop". Latin *pater* – "father" – became, on Gaulish lips, *pa'er*, and so the modern French *père*. And, in the same way, original Latin *natalis* became, first, na'al and then noel.' (*M Harrison* The Story of Christmas).

Wassail The word has been used in various senses: 1) as a greeting when giving a guest a drink or when drinking his health; 2) the drink itself, especially that drunk on Twelfth Night; 3) the custom of drinking healths from a wassail-bowl on Twelfth Night; 4) a carol or health drinking song; 5) a party at which such songs are sung or healths drunk.

Immanuel or Emmanuel From the Hebrew for 'God is with us'. The word occurs in Isaiah 7:14 'Behold a virgin shall conceive and bear a son and shall call

'Card for Emmanuel Davidson'

his name Immanuel'; and in Isaiah 8:8. In Matthew 1:22–3 the prophecy is related to the birth of Christ: 'Now all this was done that it might be fulfilled which was spoken of the Lord by the prophet, saying, Behold a virgin shall be with child and shall bring forth a son, and they shall call his name Emmanuel, which being interpreted is, God with us.'

Messiah Hebrew word meaning 'anointed', applied to a promised deliverer of the Jewish Nation and hence to Jesus of Nazareth. In the Septuagint, the most influential of the Greek versions of the Old Testament, the word was translated as *Khristos*, from which 'Christ' derives.

Alleluia Though more usually associated with Eastertide, the word does occur in some Christmas hymns. It comes from the Hebrew and means 'Praise ye Yah'. Yah is an abbreviation for Yahweh, the Hebrew name for God.

T H

The Christmas Tree

T he first historical mention of the Christmas tree is found in the notes of a certain Strasburg citizen of unknown name, written in the year 1605. 'At Christmas,' he writes, 'they set up fir-trees in the parlours at Strasburg and hang thereon roses cut out of many-coloured paper, apples, wafers, gold-foil, sweets, etc.'

We next meet with the tree in a hostile allusion by a distinguished Strasburg theologian, Dr Johann Konrad Dannhauer, Professor and Preacher at the Cathedral. In his book, *The Milk of the Catechism*, published about the middle of the seventeenth century, he speaks of 'the Christmas – or fir-tree, which people set up in their houses, hang with dolls and sweets, and afterwards shake and deflower.' 'Whence comes the custom,' he says, 'I know not; it is child's play . . . Far better were it to point the children to the spiritual cedar-tree, Jesus Christ' . . .

Though there is no recorded instance of the use of a tree in Germany before the seventeenth century, the *Weihnachtsbaum* may well be a descendant of some sacred tree carried about or set up at the beginning-of-winter festival. All things considered, it seems to belong to a class of primitive sacraments of which the example most familiar to English people is the Maypole.

C A Miles Christmas in Ritual and Tradition *1912*

'Whence comes the custom, I know not'

'A taper for every day in the year

Lighting-up time in Trafalgar Square

Prince Albert's Christmas tree at Windsor in 1841 was not, as many may imagine, the first to be seen in this country. One had been lit for a party of English children at least twenty years before, by a German of Queen Caroline's household; another, or rather three others, by the Princess Lieven, staying at Panshanger for Christmas in 1829. A fellow guest in the house was Charles Greville, who fully recorded the scene in his *Memoirs*. . . . 'It was very pretty. Here it is only for the children. In Germany the custom extends to persons of all ages.' . . . William Hewitt reported in 1840, 'It is spreading fast among the English there – pine tops being brought to market for the purpose, which are generally illuminated with a taper for every day in the year' – perhaps a numerical exaggeration.

Laurence Whistler The English Festivals *1947*

The most famous Christmas tree is that presented each year to the British people by the Norwegians in appreciation of friendship during the Second World War. King Haakon escaped to Britain after the occupation of Norway by the Germans and a Free Norwegian Government was set up in London, from whence news was broadcast regularly back to Norway. In 1947, for the first time after liberation, and every year since, a tree about 70 feet high, between 50 and 60 years old, is chosen by Norwegian foresters and ceremonially cut down in late November. It is carried free of charge from Oslo to Felixstowe on the deck of a Fred Olsen cargo vessel and hauled by road from the docks to Trafalgar Square.

Beneath an all-important slab of paving stone in the Square is a 4-foot depth of sand and soil, around which is built a temporary scaffold with which to winch the tree into its upright position. The base of the trunk is pushed hard down into the soil, a dozen wedges driven in to make it secure and then the scaffold is removed so that the tree stands unsupported as it did in the forest. On one occasion strong winds took 10 feet off the top of the tree; on another, a tree snapped neatly in half when being off-loaded at the docks. However, the people of Oslo procured a replacement in time for the ceremonial lighting in the week before Christmas. The tree is lit by 650 electric light bulbs, all white in order to simulate the traditional white candlelight. The floodlighting of the nearby National Gallery is dimmed on this occasion so as not to detract from the effect of the switching-on ceremony and to focus attention on the tree and the carol singing around its base.

Ingrid Holford

Fir tree party outside Moscow's House of Unions

Mistletoe

Christmas has long been the great occasion of decoration in English churches, and the use of holly, ivy and box at that season has lasted in an unbroken tradition through all the days of carelessness and neglect. Of all the foliage available at that cold time, mistletoe alone seems by universal agreement to be excluded from the church. It was the sacred

* Balder was the Norse God of Light, son of Odin and Frigg. The latter bound all things by oath not to harm her son, but Loki, the God of Evil, discovered that she had overlooked the mistletoe because it seemed too young. So Loki fashioned a wand of mistletoe and persuaded the blind God Hod (or Hodur) to throw it at Balder. It pierced his chest and he fell dead. Hel, the Goddess of the Dead, offered to restore him to life if all things wept for him, but Loki refused and Balder was lost. The term 'White Christ' denotes the transition from the 'Black Gods' of the Old Religion.

Plant of the Druids, which may have made the church cautious of using it; but it was also the plant which supplied the fatal shaft which slew Balder the Beautiful, and it may therefore mean that our Saxon forefathers so far clung to their ancestral myths that they would not use the death-symbol of Balder at the birth of the White Christ.* The secular frivolities connected with the mistletoe have no doubt had something to do with keeping it out of church in more recent times. It is said that there is only one instance of mistletoe being introduced in the carving of an English church and that is on a tomb in Bristol Cathedral.

The Death of Balder, from the painting by Christoffer Vilhelm Eckersberg (1783–1853) in the National Museum, Copenhagen

The Christmas decorations must be taken down before Candlemas Day,* and if but a simple leaf or berry be left in a pew some one of those who usually occupy that seat will die before another Yuletide; such at least is the belief of many, and people have been known to send their own servants to the church to sweep out their pews most carefully on Candlemas Eve.

Rev Geo S Tyack Lore and Legend of the English Church *1899*

* 2 February; the feast commemorating the purification of the Blessed Virgin Mary and the presentation of Christ in the Temple forty days after His birth.

Christmas Past

CEREMONY UPON CANDLEMAS EVE

Down with the rosemary, and so
Down with the bays and mistletoe;
Down with the holly, ivy, all
Wherewith ye dressed the Christmas Hall:
That so the superstitious find
No one least branch there left behind:
For look, how many leaves there be
Neglected, there (maids, trust to me)
So many *Goblins* you shall see.

Robert Herrick

THE CEREMONIES FOR CANDLEMAS DAY

Kindle the Christmas brand, and then
   Till sunset let it burn;
Which quench'd, then lay it up again
   Till Christmas next return.
Part must be kept wherewith to teend
   The Christmas log next year,
And where 'tis safely kept, the fiend
   Can do no mischief there.

Robert Herrick

UPON CANDLEMAS DAY

End now the white loaf and the pie,
And let all sports with Christmas die.

Robert Herrick

'. . . so many *Goblins* you shall see'

II

Music

Christmas Carols

 lthough specifically English, the carol is dependent upon foreign words for its etymology and foreign influences for its nature as understood today.

No firm agreement exists upon the origin of the word 'carol'. The favourite line traces it back through Old French *caroler* which derives from Latin *choraula*, itself deriving from Greek *choraules*, which was an aulos-player who accompanied choral dances. This line terminates at Greek *chores*, a circular dance. The French *kyrielle* also means a circular dance and may be traced forward to *carol* and backward to the Greek *Kyrie eleison* (Lord have mercy upon us), the opening words of the Roman Catholic Mass and part of the text of the Eucharist for some 1500 years.

It is evident that the dance element figures strongly in the origins of the carol. From the pagan dances of ancient Greece, through the extrovert and often ribald dances of Medieval France, carols have always possessed a decisive rhythmic lilt – a lilt too often suppressed in today's turgid, static performances of their charming melodies. Carols, it must be emphasised, are songs to be danced to; their religious connotation is usually important but their seasonal connections are of comparatively recent origin.

Originally the carol was in a strict form, alternating a repeated refrain ('burden') with stanzas. This form survives in 'God Rest Ye Merry, Gentlemen' and 'We Three Kings', but narrative and devotional carols in simple strophic (or hymn-like) form, in which the same paragraph of

A kyrielle

'. . . a decisive rhythmic lilt'

music is repeated over and over to different words (eg: 'Good King Wenceslas' and 'Away in a Manger'), have also become popular.

In the following list of twelve familiar carols, it will be noted that most have been 'manufactured', ie the music and words arose at different times and either one or both were adapted for use as a carol. An exception is 'Silent Night', which appeared through the efforts of two local worthies working under some pressure to produce a seasonal substitute for the church choir to sing while the organ was out of order. It is fortuitous that this hurried collaboration produced a carol so serene and widely loved.

One tends to hold carols in a spare corner of the mind, taking them out once per year for seasonal use. This makes them seem perpetually fresh, yet also timeless, the very essence of ancient folk heritage. As noted above, the concept of the carol is indeed ancient, and its great period of popularity in England was the 14th and 15th centuries; yet it may surprise some of us to learn how recent are the origins of many of the most 'traditional' of our carols.

In the first quarter of the 19th century the carol suffered a severe decline in popularity, but several important published collections of old and new carols were to restore interest, and it was during this period that many of today's familiar carols appeared. Popularity was further stimulated when the first festival of nine lessons and carols was inaugurated in Truro, Cornwall, in 1880. The festivals in King's College, Cambridge, began in 1918. Recordings of this annual event, together with other carol recordings made by artists from many branches of music, and the dissemination of carol services via radio and television, have made the sound of semi-religious and religious Christmas music ubiquitous during the Yuletide week; the carol is undoubtedly more popular now than ever before, even if the traditional waits have exchanged singing on snow-covered doorsteps for passive listening in centrally-heated lounges.

Away in a Manger

An American carol of recent origin. The anonymous words first appeared in 1885 in *A Little Children's Book for Schools and Families*, published in Philadelphia. The familiar tune was written by William James Kirkpatrick (1838–1921), an American composer and music director at Grace Church, Philadelphia, and published in 1895. Sometimes the words are sung to an alternative melody found traditionally in the Basque area of northern Spain.

Christians, Awake, Salute the Happy Morn

The words are by John Byrom (1691–1763), a cultured and educated man who lived with his family in Stockport, Lancashire. He it was who devised a style of shorthand upon which is based Pitman's familiar system. In 1749 he wrote the poem 'Christians, Awake' as a Christmas present for his 11-year-old daughter Dolly. The music was composed in time for Christmas 1750 by John Wainwright of Manchester and published ten years later in Sheffield (the tune is known as 'Yorkshire'). This carol was a great favourite with the English waits. Waits were minstrels employed by urban authorities to provide music for civic functions. They first appeared early in the fifteenth century and traditionally played in the streets at Christmas time for the entertainment of passers-by, some of whom showed their appreciation financially. The name 'wait' derives from their characteristic instrument, the wayte-pipe, a small but raucous wind instrument of the shawm family.

Ding Dong! Merrily on High

G R Woodward (1848–1934) is reponsible for the words of this joyful carol, but those who find the onomatopoeic nature of the first two syllables somewhat too unrestrained may choose to sing instead 'Noel' or 'Nowell'. Many references state incorrectly that the French *Noël* is synonymous with the English *carol*, but in fact it is quite a distinct type of song, being freer in form, written specifically for Christmas (carols may be designed also for Easter or for other religious occasions, or indeed may even be of a secular nature), and lacking any connection with dancing. The word *Noël* derives from *Le jour de Noël*, which equates with Latin *dies natalis*, the birthday. In English carols, the word 'noel' or 'nowell' is merely an exclamation of seasonal joy.

The music is an anonymous branle (= a rustic round dance) which was published in 1588 in a collection of French melodies called *Orchésographie* (= 'A Book of Dances') by Thoinot Arbeau (a near-anagram of his real name, Johan Tabourot, 1519–93). This *Branle de l'officiel* was adapted for use as a carol by Charles Wood (1866–1926). The last two notes of the second, fourth, and last lines ('ring-ing', sing-ing', etc) recall the emphatic leaping and stamping cadences noted in connection with 'Good King Wenceslas' (below), the mood and tempo of which should be similar to this ancient French dance.

The First Nowell

The music is possibly a descant for another carol, now unrecognised. Today it is common to raise some voices in a further descant near the end in order to introduce a climax into a tune that would otherwise end indecisively. The origins of both words and music are lost in tradition; the music was first printed in 1833 in W Sandys' *Christmas Carols New and Old*.

God Rest Ye Merry, Gentlemen

Traditional words and music, probably originating in London. First printed in 1846, the music is at least a century older, and probably very much more. A version of the tune set to patriotic words circulated in England around 1745.

Good King Wenceslas

Mid-19th century words by Dr John Mason Neale (1818–66), which replace the original, first published with the music in 1582. Those words began *Tempus adest floridam* ('The time of flowers is at hand') and indicate a lusty and joyous springtime song sung to a tune approaching in nature an abandoned fertility dance. The last two syllables of the second and fourth lines would have received emphatic treatment from singers, dancers and instrumentalists, the whole assembly stamping and clapping in riotous unison. The words 'Ste-phen' and 'ev-en' on those notes, as supplied by the Victorian Dr Neale, together with the rest of his contrived rhyme, entirely change the nature of the melody, encouraging turgid, laboured performance. The tune itself was originally a 13th century branle similar in type to that used for 'Ding Dong! Merrily on High' (see above) and was collected in *Piae Cantiones* (= Dance Songs) in 1582.

King Wenceslas (Wenzel in Germany, Václav in Bohemia, 1361–1419), King of the Romans from 1376, then King of Germany and Bohemia from 1378 to 1389, was apparently a neglectful ruler, fond of the grape, to whom the epithet 'Good' may be only doubtfully applied. There is little evidence that he would have forsaken the comfort of his castle merely to offer succour to an impecunious woodgatherer.

Hark! The Herald Angels Sing

Charles Wesley (1707–88) wrote the first version of the words for publication in *Hymns and Sacred Poems* in 1739; they were added to in 1753 by George Whitefield (1714–70) and in 1760 by M Madan (1726–90), and later still by others. In 1856 Dr William H Cummings (1831–1915), organist at Waltham Abbey, fitted them to a version of the second section of *Festgesang* (1840) by Jacob Ludwig Felix Mendelssohn (1809–47). However, the tune itself seems to have appeared first in the opera *Venus and Adonis* (first given at Drury Lane Theatre, London, on 12 March, 1715) by Johann Christoph Pepusch (1667–1752), in which it appeared as the aria 'Thus when Mars from wars returning'.

The Holly and the Ivy

The words were first printed about 1710 on an English broadside (a sheet bearing the words and carried by carol singers to encourage audience participation) and published in a collection for the first time in 1861. Their symbolism, however, is much more venerable: holly = man, ivy = woman. Alternatively, the white wood of the holly and its red berries represented the Blessed Virgin Mary mourning the spilt blood of her Son on the cross. In the words of the carol, ivy is mentioned only in passing and seems to be present at all only because it joins holly as being the only green plants in a native winter wood.

Cecil James Sharp (1859–1924), the famous English collector of folk dance and song (he gathered nearly 5000), noted down both words and music of 'The Holly and the Ivy' early this century from a Mrs Clayton in Chipping Campden, Gloucestershire, and extra words were added by a Mrs Wyatt at East Harptree, Somerset.

In Dulci Jubilo (In Sweet Jubilation)

This German/Latin macaronic carol (ie: a carol in which Latin and vernacular phrases are intermixed) is said to have been dictated by an angel to Henry Suso (died 1366), the German mystic. The earliest version published in England, similarly macaronic (Latin/English), appeared about 1540 in an assembly by John Wedderburn called *Gude and Godly Ballates* (ballad = a song for dancing). In one version of the text the second line ends 'I-O, I-O', an expression of joy from a Greek exclamation, akin to the Spanish 'olé, olé'.

The melody is a traditional German tune which appeared in *Piae Cantiones* in 1582 and was adapted by Robert Lucas de Pearsall (1795–1856). Robert Pearsall ('Lucas' commemorating his mother's maiden name; the 'de' is spurious, having been added after his death) is said to be the actual composer of the 'Cats' Duet', attributed to Rossini.

I Saw Three Ships

A carol from Newcastle-upon-Tyne, in the north-east of England, derived from 'The Three Kings of Cologne'. The Three Wise Men were Melchior, a bearded old man bearing gold, Gaspar, a young man carrying a gift of frankincense, and Balthazar, a dark-skinned traveller with his offering of myrrh. They were not kings, receiving this title only about AD 200; they were, however, the first gentiles to believe in Jesus Christ. After their death, the bodies of the three Magi were eventually taken to Constantinople (at that time called Byzantium), then to Milan, and finally to Cologne in 1162 by Frederick Barbarossa. Amongst the many versions of the words of this carol one finds 'Collein' and 'Coln' for Cologne, and the skulls (north-east English: 'crawns') of the Three Wise Men were said each to occupy one of the ships on their way up the Rhine to Cologne Cathedral. Perhaps the relics introduced too gruesome a note for a happy carol, so today the three ships are said, rather illogically, to contain 'Our Saviour Christ and his Lady', originally probably 'Our Lady'. The music, too, first printed in W Sandys' *Christmas Carols New and Old* in 1833, exists in many versions, and is mixed in some with 'London Bridge is Falling (or Broken) Down' (also from Newcastle!), with the refrain 'My Fair Lady', perhaps once 'Our Fair Lady'.

Two paradoxes remain: in bringing the relics from Milan to Cologne, why did Barbarossa choose the long sea route? And, having chosen it, why the longer one still, round the top of Scotland and thus past Newcastle, rather than along the English Channel?

Silent Night (Stille Nacht)

The words and music were written in 1818 by the parish priest of Hallein, Austria, Father Joseph Mohr (1792–1848), and the organist and schoolmaster of the village, Franz Grüber (1787–1863), for use in the church while the organ was being repaired. Grüber provided a simple accompaniment for the voices, to be playable upon any chordal instrument permitted in church; all that was available at the time was a single guitar. This hurried collaboration saved that little Tyrolean church from a silent night that Christmas eve in 1818, since unaccompanied singing was out of favour there at the time. The gentle *Siciliano* rhythm is reminiscent of the many *Pastorales* composed for Christmas concert use during the previous century and a quarter in Southern Europe and Italy.

'This hurried collaboration saved that little Tyrolean church from a silent night . . .'

The Twelve Days of Christmas

This is a secular song for Christmas rather than a carol, but it is so much a part of the festivities in Britain and America that it would be pedantic to omit it from this listing. Originally a song for Twelfth Night, it may be derived from the French troubadours, or folk poets, who sang to the self-accompaniment of lyre or lute in the 12th and 13th centuries. The melody and words similar in meaning to the French version were known in England at least by the 13th century.

The standard list of gifts enumerated in this forfeit song (a song in which the singer, if he forgets or confuses the lines, must pay a forfeit) runs as follows:

On the first day of Christmas my true-love sent to me/A partridge in a pear tree;

Second day: two turtle doves
Third day: three French hens
Fourth day: four calling birds
Fifth day: five gold rings
Sixth day: six geese a-laying
Seventh day: seven swans
*   a-swimming*

Eighth day: eight maids a-milking
Ninth day: nine ladies dancing
Tenth day: ten lords a-leaping
Eleventh day: eleven pipers piping
Twelfth day: twelve drummers
*   drumming*

The true lover's bill goes up by £1,307

By Robin Young *The Times* **24 December 1983**

The cost of true love at Christmas has increased by £1,307.08 in the past 12 months, despite an annual inflation rate at its lowest for 14 years.

The total cost of all the gifts in the song, *The Twelve Days of Christmas*, has jumped like a lord a-leaping by 26.3 per cent to reach a total of £6,277.20.

A number of economies introduced last year have been perpetuated this Christmas, but the true lover's bill is the second biggest since *The Times* first reported the calculation in 1973 – when the total was only £2,816.60.

Partridges and geese are the only items not to have risen in price. Game farms still supply live partridges at £3 each. Stuffed ones, easier to fix in pear trees, can be bought too, but would increase the bill by £348.

Pear trees are now £6.25 each. Two-tier espaliers, at £15.90, would be another £115.80. Pairs of turtle doves, a rare and protected species, are impossible to obtain, though a single stuffed one is for hire at £11.50 a week. Even white pigeons cost £18 a pair, and, the pet shop warns, it is not the right reason to be buying them.

French hens – red jungle fowl – can be hired, stuffed, at £13.80 a week. Oven-ready French chickens from Harrods would be cheaper if there was time to cook them.

Colly birds – blackbirds – cannot be legally sold, but the taxidermists' rate is £9.20 for a week's hire. Occasionally mounted road accident victims can be bought outright for £25.

The cheapest gold rings – ladies' signets in nine carat – are £18 each, and must suffice. Barnacle geese can be adopted from the Wildfowl Trust at Slimbridge, at £6 a year each. Swans, at £15 per annum, are dearer because the scheme includes a hand-painted portrait of every bird's bill pattern.

Milkmaids, even unskilled ones, qualify for the minimum agricultural wage, augmented this year to £79.20 for the five-day week. Drummers are dearer, partly because this year the Musicians' Union fixed a £5 porterage charge for their kit.

Pipers carry their own pipes and cost only the union minimum of £33 each per session at a private house. The musicians' bill would be halved if they performed in a dance hall or public house.

This year the Ballet Rambert would charge £437.40 for 11 ladies dancing on two consecutive nights, 8 per cent up on last year. The cost of leaping lords has taken a jump too, if they are to be allowed the maximum permissible expenses they could charge for mere sitting days – up to £3.90 each to £16.

The third day's French hens establish a connection with the origin of the song. More problematical are the fourth day's 'calling birds'. Most birds 'call' – a turtle dove would certainly do so – so an element of tautology is introduced. An American version recorded in 1937 has 'colored birds', again tautological with other gifts. The English 'colley birds' is given as meaning 'blackbirds' (or, less likely, the African coly, or mousebird, a medium-sized bird with a finch-like beak), which is more homely than the French *colibri* = humming bird. The fifth day's gift maintains the avian nature of the first week if 'gold rings' is read as 'goldspinks', the old Scottish name for goldfinches.

With the New Year come the humans, rustic and noisy, yet alternative versions continue with mammals which, in America, reflect the fauna of the areas in which the song is sung. Quantities differ, too, so any quantity might be found from eight to twelve for any of the following, with further permutations of species and activity virtually to taste:

hares a-running . . . hounds a-hunting . . . bulls a-roaring . . . bears a-leaping . . . wolves a-howling . . . deers a-running . . .

Robert & Celia Dearling

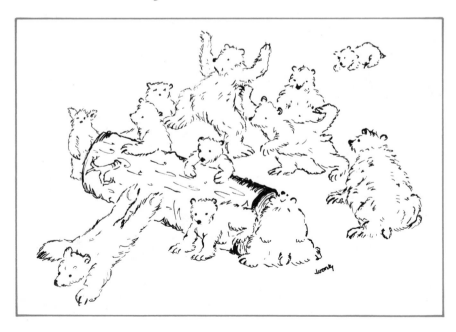

Concert Music for Christmas

The religious festival of Christmastime has inspired many a composer to write original music for the season or to take existing music (ie: carols) and adapt them for concert use. A bare listing of these works would take a disproportionate amount of space in this book – and uselessly. Instead, here are a few words to introduce an arbitrary selection of Christmasy works, some of them very familiar, others much less so.

Bach, Johann Sebastian (1685–1750): **Christmas Oratorio**

Bach prepared this cycle of six cantatas for performance during Christmas and New Year 1734–5, using a great deal of musical material from earlier secular cantatas. It does not benefit from, nor was it designed for, continuous listening since the six sections are each of similar design, yet so skilfully did Bach adapt and supplement the music that the temptation is great to proceed right through once the spell of the exciting choral writing, jubilant trumpets and daring drum solos of the opening chorus begins to work.

Johann Sebastian Bach, *left,* who was responsible for the cycle of 6 cantatas from Christmas 1734–5 and George Frideric Handel, *right,* who composed the greatest Christmas work of all, *Messiah*

Of the four soloists, the tenor takes the narrative role of Evangelist for part of the time, and the chorus is required to sing as angels in Part II, as shepherds in Part III, and as Wise Men in Part V. The orchestra includes three trumpets, two hunting horns, and four unusual oboes (two *oboi da caccia* and *two oboi d'amore* which imitate shepherd pipes in the Pastoral Symphony at the start of Part II), in addition to flutes, ordinary oboes, timpani, bassoon and strings.

Parts I—III of the Oratorio are based on St Luke 2: 1, 3–20. They were originally performed respectively on 25, 26 and 27 December, 1734. Part IV, given on 1 January, 1735, is based on the gospel account of the naming of Our Lord. Parts V and VI tell the story of the Three Wise Men and were performed respectively on 2 January and 6 January (Epiphany), 1735.

Charpentier, Marc-Antoine (c1645/50–1704): Pastorale sur la naissance de notre Seigneur Jésus Christ

Written in about 1685 for the cousin of Louis XIV, the Duchess de Guise, while Charpentier was employed by her at the Hôtel de Guide in the Marais district between 1675 and her death in 1688, this miniature opera tells the story of the nativity with simple elegance, the characters possessing added perspectives of symbolic significance.

Fry, William Henry (1813–64): Santa Claus Symphony

Fry was an American composer, born in Philadelphia, whose opera *Leonora* was premiered in New York in 1858. It was the first notable opera by an American to reach the stage. He was in Europe from 1846 to 1852, where he became a friend of Berlioz. When Louis Antoine Jullien performed Fry's 'Santa Claus' Symphony on Christmas Eve 1853 the critics were apparently unimpressed, but it is a charming and approachable major work that may well repay revival.

Handel, George Frideric (1685–1759): Messiah

This greatest of all Christmas compositions is in fact only partly for Christmas. While Part I describes events concerning the nativity, Part II deals with Christ's death, and Part III with His resurrection. Furthermore, it was only by luck that *Messiah* was written at all; and the man most closely associated with it – apart from Handel himself – had hard words to say about the music.

During the 1740–1 season, London's opera-goers appeared firmly to reject Handel: his two Italian operas produced for that season failed dolefully, and Handel considered returning in disgust to his native Germany. Fortunately, Charles Jennens, with whom Handel had worked on *Israel in Egypt* in 1738, presented the composer with another religious text, this time based on the subject of the Messiah and drawn from a wide spectrum of biblical passages. Handel immediately saw the fine quality of the setting and commenced work on Saturday, 22 August, 1741. He had completed *Messiah* by the middle of September, a mere 21 days later. Then, to Jennens's dismay, Handel took it to Ireland in November, where he was booked for a season of oratorios.

Messiah's first performance took place on 13 April 1742 at the New Music Hall, Fishamble Street, Dublin, a charity performance so successful that it was repeated a few days later. This success was duly reported back to Jennens, who had to contain himself patiently until the first London performance at Covent Garden Theatre in March, 1743. Whether through spite or pique, Jennens called some parts 'weak', and reported that Handel 'has made a fine Entertainment of it, tho' not near so good as he might & ought to have done . . . There are some passages far unworthy of Handel, but much more unworthy of the Messiah.'

Subsequently, Handel made several revisions, as was his habit with large-scale works once he had the experience of performances to guide him, and *Messiah* has been in the regular repertory ever since, appealing as strongly to those with deep musical and religious convictions as to those without.

Haydn, Franz Joseph (1732–1809): **Symphony No 26 in D minor, 'Christmas Symphony'**

Although once known by this name, Haydn's Symphony of about 1768 is in effect a tone poem representing the Passion of the Cross, and would more appropriately carry the name 'Passion Symphony' were it not that another Haydn symphony (No 49) already bears that title. A suitable alternative name for No 26 is now current: 'Lamentation'.

Hely-Hutchinson, Victor (1901–47): **Carol Symphony**

This South African-born composer was the son of the last English governor of Cape Colony. He worked in both Cape Town and England,

Left: Franz Liszt; *Above:* Amahl and
the Night Visitors

and it was while he was at the BBC in London that he composed his
Carol Symphony in 1929. The work, the first of his two symphonies,
takes its material from many of the best-known carols and is scored,
unlike its companion, for a large orchestra.

Liszt, Franz (1811–86): The Christmas Tree – Suite

Liszt wrote this charming suite between 1874 and 1876 and it was
published in Berlin in 1882. It consists of 12 movements, amongst them
descriptive pieces like 'The Shepherds at the Crib', 'Slumber Song',
and 'Evening Bells'. There are also carol arrangements and, puzzlingly,
a Hungarian Dance and a Polish mazurka. These last introduce an
autobiographical element: Liszt (a Hungarian) met the Princess Car-
olyne Sayn-Wittgenstein (of Polish origin) in 1847; she was to be his
friend and companion for many years. These two dances, and the waltz
which precedes them, recall that meeting in a kind of musical anniver-
sary/Christmas present.

Menotti, Gian Carlo (born 1911): Amahl and the Night Visitors

This American composer of Italian parentage and birth wrote this, the first television opera, in response to a commission from NBC in 1951 (he had already supplied a radio opera for NBC in 1939). The composer admitted that, faced with the commission and a Christmas deadline, he was at a complete loss, even as late as November 1951. Hieronymus Bosch's painting 'The Adoration of the Magi' chanced to catch Menotti's attention as he wandered through the Metropolitan Museum of Art in New York, and in an inspired moment he had found his subject. He set to work immediately, and the opera was ready for TV transmission in time for Christmas Eve that year.

Designed for performance by amateurs or professionals, it tells the story of a widow and her crippled son who are visited one night by the three Magi on their journey to Bethlehem. The happy outcome is, of course, a complete healing of the boy. Popular in America (it is said to be one of the most frequently performed of all 20th century operas), *Amahl* has never been acclaimed to the same extent in the UK despite a successful early TV production and the availability for many years of the work in the record catalogues.

John Antill (born 1904), one of Australia's leading composers, wrote a Christmas opera for television in 1970 entitled *The First Christmas*.

Messiaen, Olivier (born 1908): La Nativité du Seigneur

Olivier Messiaen is a French composer of deep religious conviction whose music tends towards the mystical. *La Nativité du Seigneur* for organ was composed in 1935; it is an hour-long cycle of nine meditations upon the subject of Christmas 'to honour the maternity of the Blessed Virgin'. The meditations are titled: *La Vierge et l'Enfant, Les Bergers, Desseins éternels, Le Verbe, Les enfants de Dieu, Les anges, Jésus accepte la souffrance, Les Mages,* and *Dieu parmi nous*.

Musgrave, Thea (born 1928): A Christmas Carol

This opera was premiered at Sadler's Wells Theatre in December 1981. The libretto, by the composer herself, is based on the famous story by Charles Dickens.

Vaughan Williams, Ralph (1872–1958): Five Variants of Dives and Lazarus

The ancient folk carol 'Dives and Lazarus' exists, like most folk tunes,

Ralph Vaughan Williams

in many variants. One version was used by Vaughan Williams in his *English Folk-Song Suite* of 1924, and he returned to the carol in 1939 when he was commissioned to provide a work for 'British Week' at the New York World's Fair. In the event, his work was not heard at the Fair but was given later in Carnegie Hall.

In contrast to his earlier treatment of the tune, which was for military band, the *Five Variants of Dives and Lazarus* is scored for strings alone, with harps.

Attention is also drawn to Vaughan Williams's delightful *Fantasia on Christmas Carols* for baritone soloist, choir and orchestra, written in 1912.

The Pastorale

While the shepherds watched, doubtless they played upon their rustic pipes, a stylised representation of what they played becoming something of a craze in concert rooms around the year 1700. Those shepherds' pipes were imagined to have played in a gently rocking 6/8 or 12/8 rhythm (compare the carols 'Silent Night' and 'I Saw Three Ships', both in 6/8 rhythm), with a drone bass below the melody; perhaps the instruments were bagpipes (and the imitation of bagpipes was almost certainly in Bach's mind when he introduced low toned oboes into his Pastoral Symphony in the *Christmas Oratorio* – see above). This sound and rhythm were incorporated into countless baroque concertos and classical symphonies. Every composer of the time resorted to it at some time or another, the best-known being Corelli, Torelli, and Locatelli (in concertos), Domenico Scarlatti (in several harpsichord sonatas), and Handel (the Pastoral Symphony in *Messiah*). Gaetano Maria Schiassi (1698–1754) wrote a *Christmas Symphony* for strings, and Jan Václav Antonín Stamic (1717–57) wrote another for oboes (or flutes), horns and strings. Stamic requires his shepherds to negotiate their pastorale (last movement) at a breathless *Presto*. Somewhat later (1774) Joseph Friebert (1723–99) composed a 'Christmas Symphony from Passau' for trumpets, drums and strings, in which the pastorale movement is in common-time; the lilting shepherd rhythm is entrusted to constant triplets.

It was Friebert's Symphony, and others by Christian Cannabich (1731–98) and Anton Zimmermann (1741–81), that led to Beethoven's Pastoral Symphony in which the religious connotation has given way entirely to the rustic in the slow movement (in 12/8 rhythm) which is called 'Scene by the Brook', but is restored in the last movement (in 6/8): 'Shepherd's Hymn of Thanksgiving after the Storm'.

The Play of Herod

An anonymous stylised representation of the biblical story written in the 12th century for Yuletide performance in church. Even though the prime purpose of such musical dramas (*The Play of Daniel* was another) was to educate the illiterate in the events concerning the life of Christ, the elders of the church still insisted on conducting the proceedings entirely in Latin! Clues to the musical contribution are sparse, and to the instruments and tempi of performance non-existent, yet modern reconstructions have been performed and recorded, using available data as to the practices of the time.

Robert & Celia Dearling

A Tricky Music Quiz for Christmas

QUESTIONS

1. If Rossini was born in February, 1792, and died in November, 1868, how many birthdays did he celebrate?

2. Mendelssohn's last symphony is called 'No 4'. How many did he write before it?

3. Who 'fiddled while Rome burned'?

4. Who wrote 'Invitation to the Waltz'?

5. John Cage wrote a piece entitled '4 minutes 33 seconds'. For how much of this time do the musicians actually play?

6. Who wrote Joseph Haydn's 'Toy Symphony'?

7. Why did Schubert fail to complete his 'Unfinished Symphony'?

8. Who wrote the opera 'A Midsummer Night's Dream'?

9. Who first sang the title role in Auber's opera *La muette de Portici*?

10. From what are a violinist's catgut strings made?

11. The American composer of 'Switched-On Bach', Walter Carlos, no longer writes under that name. Why?

12. How many players are required to play a baroque trio sonata?

13. Who wrote Mozart's Symphony No 3 in E flat?

14. Wolfgang Amadeus Mozart died in 1791, yet a Violin Sonata in E correctly bearing his name was composed in 1820. How come?

15. How many movements are there in Stravinsky's *Symphony in Three Movements*?

ANSWERS

1. Twenty. He was born on 29th February.

2. Sixteen: twelve unnumbered works and symphonies Nos 1, 2, 3, and 5!

3. No one. Nero played the lute.

4. No one. Weber's famous piece is called 'Invitation to the Dance'.

5. For none of it. It is a silent composition in three movements.

6. Leopold Mozart (the famous Mozart's father) wrote a seven-movement Cassation, of which movements, three, four and seven were arranged (perhaps by Haydn's brother Michael) as the 'Toy Symphony'.

7. He didn't fail. There is evidence that he probably completed it but that part of it became detached from the two familiar movements.

8. Benjamin Britten, in 1960. Mendelssohn wrote incidental music for Shakespeare's play in 1826 and 1842.

9. No one. She is mute.

10. The intestines of sheep, asses or horses.

11. He changed sex, and her name to Wendy.

12. Usually four: the two 'melody' instruments, and a bass line played by a harpsichordist and a cellist.

13. Karl Friedrich Abel (1723–87).

14. It was written by his son Franz Xaver, who changed his name to Wolfgang Amadeus after the death of his father.

15. Three.

Robert & Celia Dearling

Christmas Hit Singles and Christmas Hit Albums

What is a Christmas hit? It is a record that is a hit at Christmas time, which makes 'Return To Sender' by Elvis Presley or the soundtrack LP from the film 'South Pacific' as much of a Christmas hit as Harry Belafonte's 'Mary's Boy Child' or Slade's 'Merry Xmas Everybody'.

Christmas is the time of year when record sales are at their highest. To have a hit at Christmas is more lucrative than at any other time of the year, which is why the market from mid-November onwards is flooded with bizarre records that would never see the light of day except at a time when a large number of consumers have more money than sense. The Christmas records divide into four categories – the religious, the sentimental, the humorous and the Christmas Pop. Some records over-lap category lines. The religious category includes such songs as 'Mary's Boy Child', 'Little Drummer Boy' and 'When A Child Is Born'. The sentimental songs usually feature the younger generation: 'No-One Quite Like Grandma' and 'Two Little Boys' are prime examples. The humorous cat-egory includes such offerings as 'Ernie (The Fastest Milkman In The West)' and 'My Ding-A-Ling', which hardly fits into the mood of Christmas. Christmas Pop songs are the ones with a Christmas theme put out by the stars of the day to give them a hit at Christmas, songs like Dickie Valen-

The full list of Christmas number one hit singles is as follows:

1952 **Here In My Heart**
Al Martino

1953 **Answer Me**
Frankie Laine

1954 **Let's Have Another Party**
Winifred Atwell

1955 **Christmas Alphabet**
Dickie Valentine

1956 **Just Walkin' In The Rain**
Johnnie Ray

1957 **Mary's Boy Child**
Harry Belafonte

1958	**It's Only Make Believe** *Conway Twitty*
1959	**What Do You Want To Make Those Eyes At Me For?** *Emile Ford & The Checkmates*
1960	**It's Now Or Never** *Elvis Presley*
1961	**Tower Of Strength** *Frankie Vaughan*
1962	**Return To Sender** *Elvis Presley*
1963	**I Want To Hold Your Hand** *Beatles*
1964	**I Feel Fine** *Beatles*

tine's 'Christmas Alphabet', Slade's 'Merry Xmas Everybody' or Roy Orbison's 'Pretty Paper'.

There is of course a fifth category: those songs which are hits at Christmas despite having no religious, sentimental or humorous connection with the season whatsoever. In terms of ultimate success at Christmas – the number one hit single on Christmas Day – these songs have been most successful. Over the 32 Christmases since 1952 when the singles chart was created, only two humorous songs have held the number one spot. Only three religious songs (one song twice) and three Christmas Pop songs have been on top at Christmas, while no more than six sentimental songs can be included as chart toppers on 25 December, even if we count records like Tom Jones' 'Green Green Grass Of Home' and Renée and Renato's 1982 smash 'Save Your Love'. The charts at at least 17 Christmases have reflected no particular seasonal influence on the number one position.

In 1963 the Beatles were able to celebrate not only Christmas but the fact that they were at number one in both singles and album charts

Happy Christmas from the Stars. How many can you identify – 20 years on?

Of the 28 different acts who have topped the charts on 25 December, 16 never had another number one hit at any time.

The Christmas hit single champions are inevitably the Beatles. They had the number one single at Christmas in 1963, 1964, 1965 and 1967. Only Elvis of the other Christmas chart-toppers has managed more than one Christmas number one.

The Beatles are also the Christmas Album champions. They have been at number one in the albums charts over six Christmases, in 1963, 1964, 1965, 1967, 1968 and 1969. Apart from 'South Pacific' which was the best selling album at Christmas in 1958, 1959 and 1960, only the George Mitchell Minstrels (1961 and 1962), Elton John (1973 and 1974) and Abba (1980 and 1981) have had more than one chart topping Christmas album.

1965 **Day Tripper /We Can Work It Out** *Beatles*

1966 **Green Green Grass Of Home** *Tom Jones*

1967 **Hello Goodbye** *Beatles*

1968 **Lily The Pink** *Scaffold*

1969 **Two Little Boys** *Rolf Harris*

1970 **I Hear You Knocking** *Dave Edmunds*

1971 **Ernie (The Fastest Milkman In The West)** *Benny Hill*

1972 **Long Haired Lover From Liverpool** *Little Jimmy Osmond*

1973 **Merry Xmas Everybody** *Slade*

1974 **Lonely This Christmas** *Mud*

1975 **Bohemian Rhapsody** *Queen*

1976	**When A Child Is Born (Soleado)** *Johnny Mathis*
1977	**Mull Of Kintyre/Girls' School** *Wings*
1978	**Mary's Boy Child – Oh My Lord** *Boney M*
1979	**Another Brick In The Wall (Part II)** *Pink Floyd*
1980	**(Just Like) Starting Over** *John Lennon*
1981	**Don't You Want Me** *Human League*
1982	**Save Your Love** *Renée And Renato*
1983	**Only You** *Flying Pickets*

The full list of number one albums at Christmas since 1958 when the LP chart began is as follows:

| 1958 | **South Pacific** *Original Soundtrack* |
| 1959 | **South Pacific** *Original Soundtrack* |

The Beatles therefore topped both the singles and albums charts at Christmas four times, in 1963, 1964, 1965 and 1967. This feat was equalled by Queen in 1975, when their single 'Bohemian Rhapsody' and the album it came from, 'A Night At The Opera' both topped their respective charts.

The Beatles never recorded a specifically Christmas song. It was not until after the group had broken up that the individual members recorded Christmas songs. The first and most successful of these was 'Happy Xmas (War Is Over)' by John and Yoko, the Plastic Ono Band and the Harlem Community Choir, which was first released at Christmas 1972, and which has been a hit at four subsequent Christmases, climbing to number two in the wake of Lennon's murder at Christmas 1980. Paul McCartney's 'Wonderful Christmastime' reached number six at Christmas 1979.

The biggest selling Christmas single of all time is, of course, Bing Crosby's 'White Christmas' This is universally acknowledged as the world's biggest selling record of all time, although it was not a chart hit in Britain until Christmas 1977, shortly after Bing Crosby's death, when it climbed to number five.

The biggest selling Christmas hit single in Britain is 'Mull Of Kintyre/Girls' School' by Wings, which was at the top of the charts for nine weeks, including the week of 25 December 1977. This remains the biggest selling single in British chart history, becoming the first to sell over two million copies in Britain, and it gave Paul McCartney his fifth Christmas number one.

The first record ever to sell a million copies

Bing Crosby with Danny Kaye in a scene from Paramount's *White Christmas*. *Below*, Wings, who were responsible for the biggest-selling Christmas hit to date

1960 **South Pacific**
Original Soundtrack

1961 **Another Black And White Minstrel Show**
George Mitchell Minstrels

1962 **Black And White Minstrel Show**
George Mitchell Minstrels

1963 **With The Beatles**
Beatles

1964 **Beatles For Sale**
Beatles

1965 **Rubber Soul**
Beatles

1966 **The Sound Of Music**
Original Film Soundtrack

1967 **Sgt Pepper's Lonely Hearts Club Band**
Beatles

1968 **The Beatles**
Beatles

1969 **Abbey Road**
Beatles

1970 **Greatest Hits**
Andy Williams

1971 **Electric Warrior**
T Rex

1972	**20 All-Time Hits Of The Fifties** *Various Artists*	
1973	**Goodbye Yellow Brick Road** *Elton John*	
1974	**Elton John's Greatest Hits** *Elton John*	
1975	**A Night At The Opera** *Queen*	
1976	**22 Golden Greats** *Glen Campbell*	
1977	**Disco Fever** *Various Artists*	
1978	**Grease** *Original Film Soundtrack*	
1979	**Greatest Hits** *Rod Stewart*	
1980	**Super Trouper** *Abba*	
1981	**The Visitors** *Abba*	
1982	**The John Lennon Collection** *John Lennon*	
1983	**Now That's What I Call Music** *Various Artists*	

in Britain alone was Harry Belafonte's 'Mary's Boy Child', which topped the charts for 7 weeks over Christmas 1957. The record had the longest run at number one of any song with a Christmas theme, and became one of six songs to have reached number one in England in two different versions when 21 years later Boney M took their Christmas medley 'Mary's Boy Child – Oh My Lord' to the very top.

Although the Beatles are the Christmas hit champions, many other acts besides the Fab Four and Elvis have had more than one Christmas hit without necessarily taking these hits all the way to the top. The Christmas party medleys of the 1950s were the mainstay of each December's charts. There was Winifred Atwell's 'Let's Have A Party', 'Let's Have Another Party' (still the only medley of more than two songs to have reached the top of the singles charts), 'Let's Have A Ding Dong', 'Make It A Party', 'Let's Have A Ball' and 'Piano Party', which gave her six top ten hits and one number one in 7 years. The Big Ben Banjo Band, a studio orchestra under the direction of EMI staff producer Norrie Paramor, hit with 'Let's Get Together No. 1' and 'Let's Get Together Again' in 1954 and 1955. The Johnston Brothers missed out at Christmas 1954 with 'Join In And Sing', but made up for it in 1955 and 1956 with the hit records 'Join In And Sing Again' and 'Join In And Sing (No. 3)'. Russ Conway's increasingly complicated annual Christmas medleys from 1957 were 'Party Pops', 'More Party Pops', 'More And More Party Pops' and 'Even More Party Pops'. For Christmas, 1961, he gave up medleys and reached number seven with 'Toy Balloons'.

The rise in popularity of the long playing record helped to kill off the party medley single, but not completely. The Dave Clark Five put 'Good Old Rock'n'Roll' into the Top Ten at Christmas 1969, following it with 'More Good Old Rock'n'Roll' a year later.

The champions of Christmas humour are the Barron Knights. Their biggest hit was 'A Taste Of Aggro', their number three hit at Christmas 1978, but they also hit the festive top twenty in 1965, 1966, 1977 and 1980. The Goodies have had two Christmas hits, 'Father Christmas Do Not Touch Me' in 1974, and 'Make A Daft Noise For Christmas' in 1975. Chris Hill borrowed the Dickie Goodman technique of using short clips from hit singles to make two more, 'Renta Santa' in 1975 and 'Bionic Santa' in 1976. But on the whole, Christmas has been surprisingly not a good time for comedy hit singles, apart from Scaffold's 'Lily The Pink' in 1969, Benny Hill's 'Ernie' in 1971 and Chuck Berry's equally unChristmasy 'My Ding-A-Ling' which fell from the top spot two days before Christmas in 1972.

'Father Christmas, do not touch me'

The least well-timed Christmas hit has undoubtedly been 'I'm Walking Backwards For Christmas' by the Goons. It was first issued in June 1956, and climbed to number four, but dropped off the charts on the last day of August that year. It was re-issued in 1973, as the B-side of the re-issued 'Ying Tong Song' and although once again the Goons hit the Top Ten, the autumn equinox had not arrived before their Christmas offering disappeared a second and final time into chart obscurity.

The Beverley Sisters' version of 'Little Drummer Boy' did not enter the charts

Moira Anderson, who had an unusual chart career at Christmas 1969

until 13 February 1959, and reached number six before falling out of the charts in May. Versions of the same song, by the Harry Simeone Chorale and by Michael Flanders also entered the chart that February, and it was not until 1972 that this Christmas song was a hit at Christmas, thanks to the recording by the Royal Scots Dragoon Guards, which climbed to number 13. In 1982, David Bowie and Bing Crosby's 6-year-old duet finally turned this massively successful Christmas song into a Christmas Top Ten hit in Britain.

Pat Boone took unseasonality to the other extreme with his recording of 'April Love' which hit the Top Ten at Christmas 1957, although it did stay on the chart until May 1958. That same Christmas, Boone's version of 'White Christmas' slipped unobtrusively into the charts at 29 for 1 week.

The most obscure Christmas hit is surely Moira Anderson's 'Holy City'. The chart for 27 December 1969 was compiled but never published, and thus the world was unaware that Miss Anderson had hit the chart for the first and only time in her career at number 43. The next week, 3 January 1970, no chart was even compiled for the first time since 31 December 1954. On 10 January, a chart was both compiled and published, but 'Holy City' had disappeared out of the Top Fifty. Moira Anderson's chart career was over.

The stars have gone in for Christmas Pop, songs recorded especially for Christmas, every year since Bing Crosby showed how commercial the idea was in 1942. Mantovani's version of that 1942 hit, 'White Christmas' was in the British Top Ten at the first chart Christmas in 1952, and since then almost everybody has recorded songs for Christmas. Some have been memorable, like Elvis Presley's 'Santa Bring My Baby Back To Me' and 'Phil Spector's Christmas Album'. Some have been more forgettable.

Dickie Valentine had three consecutive Christmas hits, 'Christmas Alphabet' in 1955, 'Christmas Island' in 1956 and 'Snowbound For Christmas' in 1957. 'Christmas Alphabet' enjoys the double distinction of being the first number one hit with the word Christmas in the title, and also of remaining on the charts for only 7 weeks, the shortest chart run of any number one hit in British chart history. Until 1979, Dickie Valentine held the record of having charted with more Christmas Pop hits than anybody else, but in that year, Elvis Presley's fourth Christmas hit, 'It Won't Seem Like Christmas Without You', climbed to number thirteen to overtake Dickie Valentine. In 1980, Elvis' fifth Christmas Pop hit, 'Santa Claus Is Back In Town' increased his lead over all comers. Elvis, of course, also topped the charts with unChristmasy hits in 1960 and 1962.

Dickie Valentine liked having 'Christmas' in his song titles

In 1958, Johnny Mathis had his first Christmas hit, 'Winter Wonderland' and in 1976 he took 'When A Child Is Born (Soleado)' to number one. That was his only chart-topper, achieved 18 years and 216 days after he first hit the British charts.

In 1959, Tommy Steele's 'Little White Bull' was the sentimental Christmas smash, although it came from the film *Tommy The Toreador*, set in Spain in the summertime. In 1960, Tommy Steele tried to repeat the dose, but his 'Must Be Santa' only reached

Brenda Lee was a Christmas Pop
exception in 1962

'I Believe In Father Christmas'

number 40. The big hit of the year was
Adam Faith's 'Lonely Pup (In A Christmas
Shop)'. The sixties were generally spared of
Christmas Pop, although Brenda Lee's clas-
sic track 'Rockin' Around The Christmas
Tree' was an honourable exception in 1962,
as was Roy Orbison's 'Pretty Paper' in 1964.

The success of Slade's 'Merry Xmas Everybody' and Elton John's 'Step Into Christmas' in 1973 encouraged all and sundry to
step into Christmas Pop from then on. In
1974, Mud's 'Lonely This Christmas' and
the Wombles' 'Wombling Merry Christmas'
held down the top two chart positions,
while Showaddywaddy's 'Hey Mr Christmas' peaked at number 13. In 1975 only the
phenomenal success of Queen's 'Bohemian
Rhapsody' kept Greg Lake and 'I Believe
In Father Christmas' off the top. By 1982,
the domination of the December charts by
records with a strong connection with
Christmas was almost complete. The sentimental favourite, 'Save Your Love' was at
number one, Shakin' Stevens' 'Blue Christmas' at number two, and the David
Bowie/Bing Crosby duet medley 'Peace On
Earth – Little Drummer Boy' was at number three. Lower down there were songs
with titles such as 'Singalong-A-Santa',
'Xmas Party', 'Christmas Wrapping' and
'Christmas Rapping'. The oddity market
was covered by 'Orville's Song', 'Baa Baa
Black Sheep' by the Singing Sheep and the
reappearance of 'Birdie Song (Birdie
Dance)'. Including the re-entry of old
favourites like 'Merry Xmas Everybody'
and 'Happy Xmas (War Is Over)', as well
as Cliff Richard's first ever Christmas song,
'Little Town', no less than 19 of the Top 75
singles owed much of their commerciality

to the festive season. And yet in 1983 only two of the Top Twenty singles had a Yule-tide element, and one of those was Slade's perennial 'Merry Xmas Everybody', at number 20 on Christmas Day. What of 1984?

'White Christmas' remains after over thirty years the most recorded Christmas song, and after 'Mary's Boy Child' it is the most successful in chart terms. Two of the six hit versions of 'White Christmas' have hit the Top Ten over a period of 28 years. Only 'Little Drummer Boy' among other Christmas songs has been a Top Ten hit in more than one version, but only one of those records was a hit over the Christmas season. Two artists have had two different versions of the same Christmas song in the charts in separate years – Slade hit number one first time round with 'Merry Xmas Everybody', and in 1980 they charted again with the same song, in a re-recorded version with the Reading Choir. Johnny Mathis was at number one at Christmas 1976 with 'When A Child Is Born'. In 1981, with Gladys Knight, he charted with the same song but less successfully – just 2 weeks at 74.

Shaky – had a Blue Christmas in 1982

When Shakin' Stevens decided to record 'Blue Christmas', a number 11 hit for Elvis Presley in 1964, he created the fastest Christmas hit of all. Originally, he chose the song to sing on a Granada TV show to be broadcast on Boxing Day, and only later decided to record it. On Monday 22 November 1982, the song was recorded and the other three tracks on what was to become the Shakin' Stevens EP were mixed. On Friday 26 November, the record was in the shops and the next week it was in the charts. Bing Crosby's 'White Christmas' had taken 35 years to hit the British charts.

Elvis was successful at Christmas – but then he was successful at any time of the year

Paul Gambaccini
Jo Rice
Tim Rice
Mike Read

Detailed analysis of the Christmas charts shows one thing – the charts are no more predictable in late December than they are at any other time of the year. As those of us who have tried and failed to have a Christmas hit will agree, there is no magic formula for the instant Christmas hit. The Beatles dominate the Christmas charts, but then they did all the year round. Elvis has had more Christmas hits than anybody else, but then he's had more hits at any time of the year than anybody else. The stars who have had hits at Christmas are pretty much the same stars who have had hits all the year round, and the subject matter does not vary too much either, except that the word Christmas tends only to appear in the titles of songs issued at Christmastime (Goons always excepted). Sentiment is not only popular at Christmas, nor is humour, nor even religious themes, which can produce hits at any time of the year. The only thing that distinguishes the Christmas record from the spring, summer or autumn record is that it sells more because more money is spent in record shops in December. Quality and quantity do not often go together, so perhaps it is surprising that there have been so many excellent Christmas hits, and less surprising that there have been one or two dreadful ones. From 'White Christmas' and 'I Saw Mommy Kissing Santa Claus' in the early fifties to 'Orville's Song' and 'What Are We Gonna Get 'Er Indoors?' in the early eighties, and beyond into the future, the quality and the quantity will continue unabated, but only one single and one album a year will be able to claim the title of being the Christmas Number One.

III

Weather and the Night Sky

Christmas Weather

The winter solstice occurs on 21 December, just before Christmas. On that day the Earth is at its furthest from the Sun, and thereafter swings back into the opposite side of its elliptical track around the Sun. The southern hemisphere starts its inevitable progress towards winter, while the northern looks forward to gradually lengthening days and the approach of spring. The winter solstice has therefore always been a time of rejoicing.

However, Christmas does not necessarily imply the beginning of warmer weather. January and February, even March, are often colder than December, partly because the oceans continue to cool throughout these months.

Ice on the Thames at London Bridge, 1870

London

London at Christmas has been more often mild than cold since the middle of the 19th century. In his book *London Weather*, J H Brazell analysed the periods December 24–26 between the years 1836 and 1964. Out of these 128 years, only 17 Christmases had a mean daily temperature less than 36°F (2°C) with at least one day colder than 33°F (0·5°C), 14 of these occasions being in the 19th century. In this century similar cold Christmases happened in 1938, 1961, 1962, 1968, 1970 and 1981. 1976 was only marginally warmer. The mildest Christmas in London was in 1920, when each of the three days had a maximum temperature above 53°F (12°C).

Long-term cyclical variations in the climate, however, caused earlier centuries to be appreciably colder in winter and sometimes the Thames froze, even through London. Ice floes, unobstructed by locks, drifted down from the upper reaches of the river but were halted by the narrow arches of the bridges. Even in the tidal river the floes were then able to bond together under pressure into a continuous stretch of ice, which often looked humpy but was solid enough to bear considerable weight. Occasionally this happened at Christmas.

In the 1281–2 winter 'from this Christmas until the purification of Our Lady there was such a frost and snow as no man living could remember, where five arches of London Bridge and all Rochester Bridge were borne down and carried along on the stream, and the like happened to many bridges in England. And not long after men

WORLD TEMPERATURES AT CHRISTMAS vary widely, and average December temperatures give some idea of the disparity of conditions.

Fairbanks, Alaska suffers a chilling −9°F (−23°C) while Miami, Florida glories in 68°F (20°C).

Oslo, Norway averages 25°F (−4°C) while Lerwick, Shetland at the same latitude but warmed by the North Atlantic Drift Current, enjoys a more comfortable 39°F (4°C).

Jerusalem has an average December temperature this century of 52°F (11°C) but it could have been different in the time of our Lord.

'Down under', where Christmas happens in summer, the South Pole is remarkably warm if in December the temperature reaches 6°F (−14°C), which has happened. A normal Christmas temperature in New Zealand is about 63°F (17°C); Australian temperatures may soar to over 75° F (24° C) but that does not guarantee that the festive season is always picnic weather. In 1974, hurricane Tracy tore through Darwin, in the Northern Territory, on Christmas Day, largely demolishing the town of lightly built frame houses.

Both the named Christmas Islands, one in the Pacific Ocean near the equator and the other near Bali in the Indian Ocean, have Christmas temperatures which never vary far from 70° F (21° C).

passed over the Thames between West-minster and Lambeth dry shod.'

In 1434–5 the Thames froze between 25 December and 10 February, all the way from London Bridge to Gravesend and merchan-dise which came by ship to the Thames mouth was carried to London by land.

London Frost Fairs were occasionally held on the solidified Thames, providing enter-tainment to the people and a source of income to boatmen frozen out of their employment. Booths were set up on the ice selling songs and ballads, toys and lottery tickets, drink and refreshment, while bull-baiting and other sports took place in special arenas. Sometimes the fairs coin-cided with Christmas, one of the most spectacular being in the winter of 1683–4, in the reign of Charles II.

'From the beginning of December until the 5th of February frost congealed the River Thames to such an extent that another city, as it were, was erected thereon. Where, by the great number of streets and shops, with their rich furniture, it represented a great fair with a variety of carriages and diver-sions of all sorts; and near Whitehall a whole ox was roasted on the ice.' The King himself visited the fair but died just one day after the ice started to break up.

Cold winters still happen, as in 1962–3, when the Thames froze in many places in the upper non-tidal reaches. Through Lon-don, however, waste heat from power sta-tions and industry keeps river temperature well above freezing point and wide bridge spans give easy thoroughfare for any ice floes which may drift down. Frost fairs in London are now part of history.

Top: Frost Fair on the Thames in the reign of Charles II; *Above:* Skating in Hyde Park in 1857

Christmas weather in the British Isles, kept damp by proximity to the Atlantic, is more often white with fog than with snow. Charles Dickens was being thoroughly realistic when he set the scene for his *Christmas Carol* in 'cold, bleak, biting weather; foggy withal . . . pouring in at every chink and keyhole, and so dense that the houses opposite were mere phantoms.' Three successive Christmases were foggy in London this century, 1942–4, although temperatures then were not particularly low. In 1981, however, fog was combined with bitter cold and travelling conditions

UNITED KINGDOM DECEMBER TEMPERATURES range modestly, from just over 45° F (7° C) at Plymouth, Devon and at Malin Head, N Ireland, to about 41° F (5° C) at Manchester and nearly 39° F (4° C) at Aberdeen, Scotland. Statistics such as these, however, averaged over a period of 30 years, camouflage the occasional very cold spells. December, 1981, was severe, Aberdeen being 6·3° F (3·5° C) degrees colder than usual. Braemar, always having lower temperatures than other Scottish localities, suffered its coldest December since records began there in 1855. Over the 3-day Christmas period the average maximum temperature was just below freezing point, while the average minimum was 3·7° F (−15·7° C). From midnight to midnight on Christmas Day the temperature never rose above 12° F (−11·1° C).

The Automobile Association to the rescue

were extremely treacherous. Car windscreens became coated with ice as fog, below freezing temperature, froze on to the glass, and roads were often glazed into ice rinks.

White Christmases

Snow at Christmas is virtually unknown in latitudes lower than 40°, except on high mountains. In polar regions, on the other hand, there is no precipitation other than snow; only a little at a time, but lying refrigerated year after year to compact into deep ice sheets.

In temperate latitudes, mountainous regions often have snow at Christmas, the heaviest falls often being in the Rocky Mountain spine running down the western side of North America. In one 5-day period starting on Boxing Day 1955, the Thomson Pass in Alaska had a snow fall of 175 in (4455 mm) – a record for that short period and about 35 per cent of the normal snowfall for 1 year.

White Christmases in the low-lying areas of the United Kingdom are infrequent and therefore a matter for gambling. Bookmakers watch anxiously on the roof of the London Weather Centre for any snow flakes which might earn or lose them money! More practically, insurance companies provide policies for parties, usually travelling by coach, who might be unable to reach theatres, pantomimes, etc, because of fog, snow or ice. The risk is particularly pronounced when the travellers must cross high ground like the Pennines, the Peak District or the Welsh Mountains, which quickly become impassable in snow. Abandonment policies, however, must be taken out at least 14 days before the events to be covered, that is to say outside the range of detailed forecasts issued by the Meteorological Office.

Within living memory crippling snowfalls in the south of England at Christmas have occurred in 1927, when the blizzard started on Christmas night and continued all Boxing Day; in 1938 snow started on 18 December and continued almost daily until December 26; and in 1962 the snow started suddenly on Boxing Day, snowing up many travellers going to parties. The 1981 Christmas was white over most of the country, but the snow had mainly fallen beforehand. London had about 4 inches of lying snow on Christmas day in 1968 and small amounts also in 1970. The Christmas card image of a white Christmas seems odd in view of the foregoing statistics. However, because of their rarity white Christmases are impressive and memorable, and fertile backdrops for authors' imagination. Charles Dickens was a young journalist of 24 in 1836 when the first of his *Pickwick Papers* was published. By the time he wrote the episode about shovelling away snow and skating on the ice he would have experienced the Christmas of 1836, one of the most notorious blizzards in the south of England and the only one to result in a fatal avalanche in a populated area. A Mr Thomson gave a vivid account of his experiences to the *Sussex Express*.

He set out about 2 pm on Christmas Eve to travel from London to his home in Sussex. The weather was overcast and gloomy, but there was little snow on the road till he reached Ashdown Forest, where driving

Christmas weather featured in the writings of Charles Dickens

conditions became very difficult. Snow was blowing in strong wind, the horses could hardly keep upright and deep snow drifts were forming. Thomson eventually reached Lewes about 11 pm, but, when he opened his front door, snow, compacted hard against it, fell inwards and it was an hour before he could again shut the door.

Meanwhile in the eastern part of Lewes, the wind was screaming over the top of the Downs and eddying backward at the edge of the steep Cliffe Hill, which had been excavated for chalk. Snow packed into the cliff face until it formed a ledge 10–15 ft thick projecting, unsupported, above a row of houses 200 feet below. Such a snow feature is called a cornice and is well known and dreaded in countries where snow is an annual occurrence. It was not a hazard recognized by the inhabitants of Lewes. By

The Snowdrop Inn stands on the site of the fatal avalanche of 1836

daylight on Christmas Day the snow had stopped and the overhanging wave of snow, unsupported by anything other than the self-adhesive properties of its own ice crystals, was admired for its beauty and few voices were raised in warning. On Boxing Day a large mass of snow fell from the cliff into an adjacent timber yard, and on the morning of 27 December the sun shone. At about 9.30 am fissures were noticed in the cornice above the houses and a young man implored the inhabitants to flee. They refused and some minutes later the cornice collapsed and the avalanche of snow hit the houses. When the airborne flakes had settled nothing could be seen but a mound covered by snow, and it took all day to dig out the fifteen buried people, of whom eight were dead. The Snowdrop Inn now stands on the original site but the cliff has been excavated further back so that any future cornice could fall to safety into a pit.

Ingrid Holford

The Christmas Sky

Christmas is with us once more – and so is the Christmas sky. There is no Moon to drown the light of the stars; the Moon was new on 22 December, so that the stars can shine out in their full splendour.

One star you won't see, I'm afraid, is the Star of Bethlehem. On countless occasions I have been asked what it was. The answer is that I don't know, and neither does anybody else. It was certainly not an ordinary star or planet; it cannot have been due to planets so close together in the sky that they merged into one brilliant point; if it had been a nova or exploding star, it would have remained on view for some time, and astronomers of the day would have mentioned it. Neither can we attribute it to our old friend Halley's Comet, which came into view a dozen years earlier and was well out of the way by the time of Christ's birth (which was probably around 4 BC). So the mystery remains, and presumably always will.

But if you look to the west after sunset, you will see the magnificent planet Venus, which has often been confused with the Star of Bethlehem. Venus is brighter than anything else in the sky apart from the Sun and the Moon, and it cannot possibly be mistaken. Of course, it is not a star; it is a planet, about the same size as the Earth, and rather closer to the Sun than we are. It seems so outstanding partly because it is comparatively close (at its nearest it can approach us to within 25 million miles, which astronomically is not far), and partly because it has a dense, cloudy atmosphere which reflects the sunlight well. It is hardly surprising that the ancients named it after the Goddess of Beauty. Alas, Venus isn't really a friendly world. It has a fiercely hot surface, at a temperature of at least 900 degrees Fahrenheit; its 'air' is dense and unbreathable; its clouds contain a great deal of the dangerous substance we call sulphuric acid, and on the planet's surface there is almost continuous thunder and lightning, together with volcanic eruptions in some areas. I don't expect anyone to go there!

Of the other planets, Jupiter is visible above the south-western horizon for a very short time, but it is so close to the Sun in the sky that you may not see it. Mars is also an evening object, but not very bright, even though its redness marks it out at once. Saturn, with its wonderful ring-system, rises shortly before the Sun, but is not favourably placed. Incidentally, Halley's Comet is approaching the Sun; but it is still faint and it will not become visible with small telescopes much before the beginning of December, 1985. Frankly it will not be conspicuous at any time; to see it really well, we must wait for it to come back again in the year 2062.

Of the winter stars, pride of place must go to Orion the Hunter. It is easy to find Orion in the south-east after sunset. Its pattern is unmistakeable, and you will note its two leading stars, Betelgeux on the upper left-hand corner of the constellation and Rigel in the lower right. They are stars of very different kinds. Betelgeux is a huge Red Giant; it is big enough to swallow up the whole path of the Earth round the Sun, and its diameter is around 250 000 000 miles. It shines 15 000 times more powerfully than the Sun, but even this is not much compared

Diagram 1

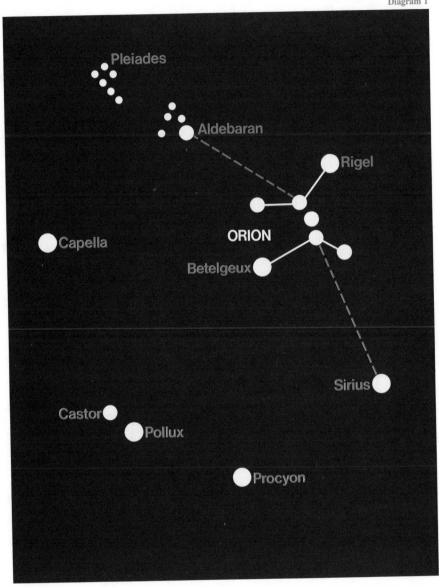

Diagram 2

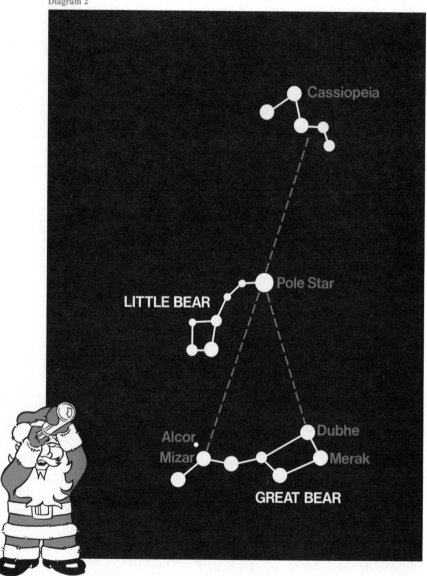

with the brilliant white Rigel, which is the equal of 60 000 Suns. Obviously, Rigel is a long way from us. Its light takes about 900 years to reach us, so that we are now seeing Rigel not as it is today, but as it used to be in the time of William the Conqueror.

The three stars which make up Orion's Belt are hot and white. Below them you will be able to make out the misty Sword, which is a nebula – that is to say, a vast cloud of dust and gas, inside which fresh stars are being born. Binoculars show it well. Several thousands of millions of years ago, our Sun must have been born inside a nebula of this kind.

Diagram 1: Follow down the line of Orion's Belt, and you will come to the most brilliant star in the sky – Sirius, the Dog-Star. It twinkles strongly, not because it is really doing so, but because its light is being 'shaken around' as it passes through the Earth's unsteady atmosphere. All stars twinkle to some extent, but Sirius shows it particularly strongly, because of its brightness and because it stays rather low over the horizon in England. Actually it is not nearly so powerful as Rigel or Betelgeux; it is only as luminous as 26 Suns, but it is one of the nearest of all the stars. Its distance from us is around 50 million million miles.

Now go back to Orion's Belt and follow the line upward. You will come to another red star, Aldebaran in the Bull, from which extends a sort of V-formation of faint stars making up the cluster which we call the Hyades. Beyond them, look for the Pleiades or Seven Sisters. This is another cluster; you should be able to make out at least seven separate stars, but binoculars or telescopes show many more.

Almost straight overhead you will see another brilliant star: Capella in the constellation of the Charioteer – yellow like the Sun, but much more luminous. Also in Orion's retinue are the two Twins, Castor and Pollux, and the leader of the Little Dog, Procyon. If you look at the Twins you will see that while Pollux is orange, Castor is white. In fact, Castor is not a single star; it is a system made up of six stars, four bright and two faint – a sort of family gathering.

Now leave Orion and look rather low in the north. There you will see the Great Bear, sometimes called the Plough. It is not so brilliant as Orion, but it never sets, so that you can always see it somewhere whenever the sky is sufficiently dark and clear. Look at Mizar, the second star in the Bear's tail; it has a much fainter star, Alcor, close beside it. If you have a small telescope, you will find that Mizar itself is made up of two stars, one rather brighter than the other.

Diagram 2: Use the Pointers, Merak and Dubhe, to find the Pole Star in the Little Bear, which lies so close to the north pole of the sky that it hardly seems to move at all. Then trace the Little Bear itself, curving down over the Great Bear's tail; and you can also locate the W-formation of stars making up Cassiopeia, which, like the Bears, never sets. And when the Moon is out of the way, look for the lovely band of the Milky Way, stretching across the sky from one horizon to the other, passing from near Orion and the Twins through Cassiopeia and down to the west. It is made up of stars, as you will see if you use your binoculars, but the stars are not really crowded together; we are simply seeing many stars in almost the same direction.

So there is plenty to see in the sky this Christmas; even without a telescope or pair of binoculars you have an amazing selection of wonderful sights – even if we can't produce the Star of Bethlehem!

Patrick Moore

IV

Food and Drink

Roast Turkey – Recipes New and Old

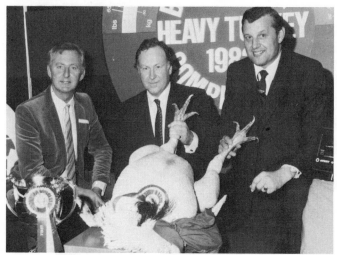

The heaviest and most expensive turkey – dressed weight 78 lb 14¾ oz, the greatest ever recorded – made £3000 at auction on 15 December 1982

* Although many people do stuff both ends of the turkey, overfilling can result in the bird not being thoroughly cooked. Great care should be taken not to put too much stuffing in the body cavity. The stuffing can be cooked separately and an onion or lemon placed in the bird during cooking.

Prepare your turkey for roasting the day before. Stuff each end of the bird* and rub lavishly all over with at least ¼ lb butter or margarine. Wrap up in well buttered foil and put in a roasting tin. On Christmas Day preheat the oven to Gas Mark 3/325°F/160°C (unless you are doing your roast potatoes in advance). Put the turkey low down in the oven and cook for 2½–3 hours for a 6–8 lb (2·5–3·5 kg) bird, 3–3¾ hours for an 8–14 lb (3·5–6·0 kg) bird and 3¾–4¼ hours for a 14–18 lb (6·0–8·0 kg) bird. Three quarters of an hour before it is ready, unwrap the foil to expose the turkey so that it will brown, and pour a glass of dry vermouth or white wine over it.

After you have transferred the turkey to a carving board make the gravy. Blend 1 rounded teaspoon (2×5 ml spoon) of arrowroot or cornflour with a little water and stir into the pan juices. Let this bubble over the heat until thickened and season to taste. Serve the gravy with the turkey, accompanied by cranberry sauce and bread sauce.

from Cooking for Christmas *by Josceline Dimbleby*

T he best way to roast a turkey is to loosen the skin on the Breast of the Turkey, and fill it with Force-Meat, made thus: Take a Quarter of a Pound of Beef Sewet, as many Crumbs of Bread, a little Lemon peel, an Anchovy, some Nutmeg, Pepper, Parsley and a little Thyme. Chop and beat them all well together, mix them with the Yolk of an Egg, and stuff up the Breast; when you have no Sewet, Butter will do; or you may make your Force-Meat thus: Spread Bread and Butter thin, and grate some Nutmeg over it; when you have enough roll it up, and stuff the Breast of the Turkey; then roast it of a fine Brown, but be sure to pin some white Paper (i.e. grease-proof) on the Breast till it is near enough. You must have a good gravy in the Dish, and Bread-Sauce, made thus: Take a good piece of Crumb, put it into a pint of Water, with a blade or two of Mace, two or three Cloves, and some Whole Pepper. Boil it up five or six times, then with a spoon take out the Spice you had before put in, and then you must pour off the Water (you may boil an Onion in it if you please) then beat up the Bread with a good Piece of Butter and a little Salt.

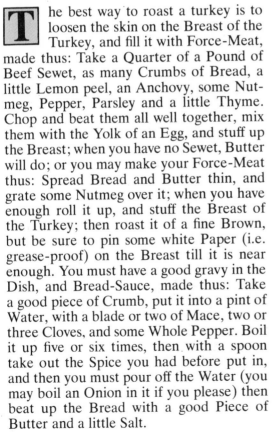

Mrs Glasse The Art of Cookery made Plain and Easy *1755*

Turkey Talk

The Turkey is surely one of the prettiest presents which the Old World has received from the New. Superlatively knowing persons maintain that the Romans were addicted to the Turkey, that it was served at Charlemagne's wedding-feast, and that therefore it is false to praise the Jesuits for this most savoury of imports. Let us silence such dealers in paradox with a twofold refutation:

1 The French name of the bird, which being coq d'inde, clearly betrays its origin: for at first America was always known as the Western Indies;
2 The appearance of the bird, which is clearly outlandish.

A scholar could make no mistake about it. Nevertheless, convinced already as I was, I have been at some pains to investigate the subject, and here are my conclusions:

1 That the Turkey appeared in Europe towards the end of the seventeenth century;

2 That it was imported by the Jesuits, who bred it in large numbers, particularly on one of their farms in the neighbourhood of Bourges;

3 That from there it gradually spread over the whole of France; and hence it was that in many dialects the word for Turkey became and still is jesuite;

4   That America is the only place where the Turkey has been found wild and in a state of nature (there are none in Africa);

5   That in North America, where it is very common, they rear it either from eggs found in the forest and hatched in captivity, or from young birds caught wild; so reared, it is nearer to its natural state, and retains its primitive plumage.

The case is proved to my complete satisfaction, and I here give thanks to the good Fathers for their enterprise in this matter as well as in another, namely the importation of quinine, which is called in English, Jesuit's-bark.

J A Brillat-Savarin (1755–1826)

Brillat-Savarin was not altogether right. The *Encyclopaedia Britannica* (1963 edition) has the following to say: '*Meleagris galloparvo*, the North American turkey, was originally native to the south western, midwestern and eastern United States, southern Ontario and nearly all of Mexico. This species is the source of all domesticated turkeys which are found in almost all countries of the world ... Turkeys had been domesticated by the Aztec Indians of southern Mexico prior to the European discovery and were taken to Spain about 1519. From Spain the stocks spread throughout Europe, reaching England about 1541.' From the edition of 1911 the following information may be gleaned:

'How (the turkey) came by this name has long been a matter of discussion for it is certain that the valuable animal was introduced to Europe from the New World, and its introduction had nothing to do with Turkey or the Turks, even in the old and extended sense in which that term was applied to all Mahommedans. But it is almost as unquestionable that the name was originally applied to the bird which we know as the guinea-fowl, and there is no doubt that some authors curiously confounded the two species. As both birds became more common and better known, the distinction was gradually perceived and the name "turkey" became restricted to that from the New World – possibly because of its repeated call-note – to be syllabled *turk, turk, turk*, whereby it may almost be said to have named itself . . . The Turkey, so far as we know, was first described by Oviedo (1478–1557) in his *Sumario de la natural historia de las Indias*, said to have been published in 1527.'

So that, you may suppose, is that. However, the equally prestigious *Oxford Dictionary of English Etymology* has an altogether different tale to tell: 'The name of the country (the land of the Turks), (was) first applied to the African bird (the guinea-fowl) probably because it was originally brought from New Guinea by the Portuguese through Turkish dominions, and later applied to the American bird to which it became restricted, and to which *Meleagris*, the name by which the guinea-fowl was known to the Greeks and Romans, was attached by Linnaeus in his classification.'

However, as Brillat-Savarin says, there seems to be no doubt about the origin of the French word for 'turkey'. Because the explorers of the late fifteenth and early sixteenth centuries believed that by sailing west they would reach India, the first islands they discovered became known as the West Indies, wherefrom the French first called the bird the *Coq d'Inde*, whence *Dindon*.

T H

Oxtail Cooked with Guinness

Dice all the peeled vegetables and have them ready in a bowl. Put the seasoned flour into a plastic bag and shake the pieces of oxtail in it two by two so they are all coated with the flour.

Heat the fat in a frying pan and brown the pieces of oxtail all over. Transfer them to a large casserole with a slotted spoon or spatula.

In remaining fat brown all the vegetables and add them to the casserole. Gently fry any remaining flour until brown and gradually stir in the previously heated bouillon, scraping to amalgamate all the little bits left from frying.

2 oxtails cut into joints.
2 oz well-seasoned flour (salt, pepper, mustard).
2 × 15 oz cans of Guinness, 2 oz dripping or butter, bouquet garni (thyme, bayleaf & parsley), 2 medium onions, 4 sticks of celery, 2 turnips, 6 carrots, ½pt or ¾pt of bouillon (made with stock cube if none available), seasoning to taste.

Add the Guinness (you may have to do this in two lots) and then pour the mixture over the oxtail, vegetables and bouquet garni, stirring gently to mix all together.

Bring the casserole to simmering point on top of the stove, cover and cook in the oven at Gas Mark 1 (300°F/145°C) for four hours.

Strain oxtail and vegetables and leave gravy overnight in the refrigerator – when the fat will rise and settle on the top. Remove the fat but keep for further dripping to fry things in.

Combine the gravy and oxtail and heat again – taste for seasoning – at this point it tastes very odd before the seasoning – (salt & pepper – maybe a touch of Worcester sauce) and reheat in the oven until hot.

Serve with mashed potatoes and peas.

Jennifer Paterson

Spicy Beef and Guinness Pie (Serves 6–8)

A golden pie which looks and tastes extra-special. It is most suitable for one of your festive meals as it can be prepared well beforehand and will only need putting into the oven to bake. If you have an aversion to prunes do not be put off – they disintegrate in the stout and produce the most delicious, rich, dark sauce. The juniper berries are optional but can be found in most delicatessens and will add tantalisingly to the flavour. Allspice is best ground from whole berries but you can also buy it ground (just to muddle you it is

For the easy flaky pastry:

8 oz (200 g) plain flour

good pinch salt

6 oz (150 g) from an 8 oz block frozen butter or margarine

sometimes known as Pimento or Jamaica pepper). If you cannot find allspice use more nutmeg and two more cloves. For the top you can use packet puff pastry if you like but the easy flaky pastry is very little trouble and beautifully crisp. Make your pastry first or while the pie filling is cooking.

To make the pastry, sift the flour and salt into a bowl. Put a grater into the bowl on top of the flour. Hold the frozen butter in its wrapping and coarsely grate off 6 oz (three-quarters of the block). With a palette knife mix the fat into the flour until crumbly. Now add the water gradually, mixing again with the knife and then gather the dough up with your hands into a ball. Wrap in foil or polythene and put in the fridge for at least an hour.

Heat the oven to Gas Mark 1 (275° F/140° C). Crush the allspice and cloves together in a pestle and mortar or in a coffee grinder, add the juniper berries and crush roughly. Heat the oil in the bottom of an iron casserole. Put the crushed spices together with the grated nutmeg and chopped garlic into the hot oil and stir over the heat for ½ minute. Add the beef and just seal all over for 2–3 minutes over a high heat. Stir in the stout and ½ cup water. Remove the stones from the soaked prunes and add.

Bring to the boil and then cover the dish and cook in the oven at Gas Mark 1 (275° F/140° C) for an hour. (Make the pastry now if you have not already.) Then add the carrots and continue cooking for a further 1–1½ hours until the meat is tender. Season to taste with salt and black pepper. Blend the arrowroot with a spot of water

6 tablespoons (6 × 15 ml spoon) very cold water – preferably chilled in the fridge

For the glaze – 1 egg yolk

For the pie filling:

1 teaspoon (5 ml spoon) whole allspice berries

6 cloves

1 teaspoon (5 ml spoon) juniper berries (optional)

1 tablespoon (15 ml spoon) oil

¼–½ whole nutmeg – grated

2–3 large cloves garlic – chopped finely

2 lb (800 g) lean stewing beef – chopped in cubes

½ pt bottle Guinness

8 oz (200 g) large prunes – soaked in water overnight

1 lb (400 g) carrots – cleaned and sliced

salt, black pepper

2 teaspoons (2 × 5 ml spoon) arrowroot

and stir in. Bubble for a minute or two on top of the stove. Then pour into a 2½ pt pie dish and leave until cold.

When the filling is cold, roll out the pastry on a floured surface to roughly the size and shape of the pie dish. Moisten the edge of the dish and lay the pastry on top. Cut round the edges and press down lightly. Roll out the trimmings and use to make a pattern, or cut-out letters to read 'Happy Christmas'! Cover the pastry loosely with plastic film or foil and put the complete dish in the fridge until the next day, or in the freezer (if the freezer, remember to defrost before baking).

To bake, heat the oven to Gas Mark 7 (425° F/220° C). Brush the pastry all over with egg yolk and cook in the centre of the oven for about 20 minutes until a rich golden brown. Serve with a green salad.

from Cooking for Christmas *by Josceline Dimbleby*

Mr Guinness's Christmas Pudding

Mix all the dry ingredients in a basin. Add lemon juice, egg, milk and Guinness. Turn into a 2½ pint (1 litre) basin. Cover with a pudding cloth or greaseproof paper or foil. Leave overnight. Steam the pudding for 7½ hours. Let the pudding cool and then recover. Store in a dry cool place. Steam for a further 2 to 3 hours before serving.

Just Imagine . . .

The 1981 census records that there are 16 720 168 households in England. Let's imagine that every family has a Christmas pudding. We need to find the weight of one Christmas pudding by adding up the amounts of all the dry ingredients and adding 250 g to the total to allow for the liquids used in the mixture.

142 g + 113 g + 113 g + 142 g + 285 g + 142 g
= 680 g
+ 250 g for liquids
Total 680 g + 250 g = 930 g

This is near to 1000 g or 1 kg and in our calculations we are going to assume that each pudding weighs 1 kg. If each of the 16 720 168 families in England put their pudding mixtures together to make a giant pudding we would have a pudding weighing 16 720 168 kg. We can convert this into tonnes:

$$\frac{16\ 720\ 168}{1000} = 16\ 720\cdot168 \text{ tonnes}$$

How many currants?

Each Christmas pudding contains 4 oz (113 g) of currants. Try counting out 113 g of currants. We found that we had a total of 650 currants. If there are 650 currants in one pudding how many would there be in the giant pudding?

For your calculation

16 720 168
    650 ×
_____

In our experiment 140 currants placed end to end cover a distance of 1 metre. What would be the length of the line of currants from one Christmas pudding?

**Ingredients for
Mr Guinness's
Christmas Pudding**

5 oz (142 g) fresh breadcrumbs

4 oz (113 g) soft brown sugar

4 oz (113 g) currants

5 oz (142 g) sultanas

1 oz (28 g) chopped peel

5 oz (142 g) shredded suet

¼ teaspoon (1·25 ml) salt

½ teaspoon (2·5 ml) mixed spice

rind of ½ a lemon (grated)

2 teaspoons (10 ml) lemon juice

1 large egg (beaten)

⅛ pint (75 ml) milk

¼ pint (142 ml) Guinness

Do you think the currants could stretch around the Equator?

The Earth's closest neighbour in space is the Moon at a mean distance of 376 284 km surface to surface.

How far will the currants from the giant Christmas pudding reach out into space towards the Moon?

Calculation:

$$\frac{16\ 720\ 168 \times 650}{140 \times 1000} = 376\ 284$$

Reaching Around the Equator

The circumference of the Earth at the Equator is 40 075 02 km

How many times (approx) would the currants from the giant pudding reach around the Earth?

Calculation:

$$\frac{16\ 720\ 168 \times 650}{140 \times 1000 \times 40\ 075}$$

Phew!

The *Guinness Book of Records* gives the weight of the world's largest Christmas cake as 31·69 tonnes.

How many times heavier is our Just Imagine giant Christmas pudding than the world's largest cake?

Calculation:

$$\frac{16\ 720 \cdot 168}{31 \cdot 69} = \text{——— times as heavy}$$

Use reference books to find objects that have the equivalent weight to our Just Imagine giant Christmas pudding. Would it be, for example, about the same weight as the Royal Navy's newest aircraft carrier HMS *Invincible*?

Try to undertake all your calculations first without the aid of a calculator and then with a calculator. Record the time taken for each of your calculations. Don't forget there are many more possibilities for your Christmas calculations; the number of Christmas cards posted and working out the average number of cards received by each family is one possibility. Calculating the cost of the postage is another!

Leonard Marsh

Seasonal Drinks

Whene'er a bowl of punch we make,
Four striking opposites we take:
The strong, the weak, the sour,
the sweet,
Together mixed most kindly meet:
And when they happily unite
The bowl is pregnant with delight.

In spite of this rhyme, which I found in an old cookery book, the word punch comes from the Indian word *panch* meaning five – ie, five ingredients. However, there are all sorts of punches, with varying numbers of ingredients.

from Cooking for Christmas *by Josceline Dimbleby*

Christmas Carol Punch

(For twenty persons)

Dissolve a quarter of a pound of sugar in a pint of boiling water, and pour into a China bowl, which may be one decorated with some formal or pleasing pattern, as fancy may dictate, or piety direct. Add the juice of two lemons, with the rinds, half a pint of ginger brandy, one bottle of Jamaica rum, a few sticks of cinnamon, a handful of cloves, and six orange slices.

Allow to simmer, and serve hot in punch glasses. A silver ladle is customary.

Recipe by H McElhone

Mulled Ale

Make some ale quite hot, and add a little

grated nutmeg or mixed spice. For each quart of ale beat up half a dozen eggs and mix with a little cold ale, then pour the hot into it and empty from vessel to vessel several times to prevent curdling, for the space of a *Pater* and five *Aves*.

Stir over the fire till sufficiently thick, add a piece of butter or a dash of brandy, and serve with dry toast.

R M

HP *The Christmas Wine*

V

Mail, Coins and Stamps

Christmas Mail

Many countries have organised special postal facilities to handle Christmas mail and a wide range of distinctive postmarks has been produced.

At one time Britain's Post Offices actually delivered mail on Christmas Day itself, and it was customary for people to receive their cards on Christmas morning. This practice, however, placed an intolerable burden on the postal staff and by the end of the 19th century the Post Office was urging people to post their cards in advance. As the public persisted in the desire to get cards on the day itself, the Post Office eventually devised a scheme to make this possible while, at the same time, relieving the pressure which built up on Christmas Eve. The scheme was tried experimentally at Rochdale in December, 1902, and the public were encouraged to post their cards well in advance, with the promise that they would be sorted and held for delivery on Christmas Day. A special postmark was used, inscribed POSTED IN ADVANCE FOR DELIVERY ON CHRISTMAS DAY. This scheme was such a success that it was extended to other towns in Cheshire and Lancashire the following year. Eventually the advance posting system, with its distinctive postmark, was operating in about forty towns, mainly in England, but including several in Scotland, Ireland and the Isle of Man. After the initial enthusiasm had worn off, however, the public reverted to their old practices and by 1909 the advance posting scheme was being regarded as more trouble than it was worth, so the Post Office quietly

Three young wise men delivering Post Office first-day covers bearing the Christmas 1979 stamps to Archbishop Donald Coggan at Church House, Westminster (See previous page)

dropped it. Judging by the rarity of the postmarks – in some cases no actual examples have yet been found, though the marks are known to have been issued – the public do not seem to have supported the scheme as widely as the Post Office had hoped.

Canada operated a somewhat similar system between 1926 and 1945. Though special postmarks like the British were not used, machine cancellation was applied in red instead of black, to enable the sorters to distinguish the Christmas mail. This scheme, which eventually operated in Winnipeg, Toronto, Montreal, Halifax, St John and Barrie, Ontario, was backed by slogan postmarks urging the public to USE ADVANCE POSTING FOR CHRISTMAS.

Most countries, however, have contented themselves with slogans exhorting the public to post early for Christmas. Britain began using such slogans in 1925 and variations on this theme continued till 1966 when 'Post your Christmas cards by the 20th December' was substituted. This continued till 1970 when the public were asked PLEASE POST CARDS IN BUNDLES. Having tried to educate the public in these matters for almost half a century the Post Office then gave up and since then the slogans have taken the form of Christmas greetings, a bilingual version being used in Wales.

Since 1964 a number of towns have sponsored individual slogans, usually alluding to their Christmas shopping facilities and seasonal attractions. A few have even used Christmas greetings to drum up goodwill at a time when most people are thinking of booking holidays for the following summer, and in recent years slogans have advertised pantomimes. Not all slogans, however, have emphasised the more commercial aspects of Christmas. The Tenovus anti-cancer campaign has used this medium to thank those who have supported it, while slogans were used in 1972 to publicise the Save the Children campaign.

Slogans urging the public to post early for Christmas have been used in many other countries. While the United States uses a picture of Santa Claus with a brimming shopping bag to hammer home the message SHOP EARLY FOR CHRISTMAS, neighbouring Canada has for many years used the slogan PUT CHRIST BACK INTO CHRISTMAS. Slogans with Christmas greetings from the Post Office originated in Italy in the 1950s and have now spread world-wide.

Several countries also operate a scheme enabling children to communicate with Santa Claus. In Britain letters written to fantasy addresses, such as Reindeerland, Toyland or Snowland, find their way to a special section of the Post Office in Edinburgh where Santa and his helpers duly send out cards to his admirers. These cards are contained in envelopes franked by a special postmark that shows the indefatigable saint jingling across the night sky, the Paid dater die bearing the name of Reindeerland. Letters addressed to Santa at the North Pole are required, under Universal Postal Union regulations, to be forwarded to their destination, since it is a real place. In this instance responsibility for replying falls upon the Greenland Post Office who used to welcome the inclusion of a small postal order to defray the cost of the reply!

In France children who write in receive in due course a charming reply from Père

Santa Claus with his updated sleigh

Noël. New Zealand's Post Office operates a Santa Claus service free to its youthful correspondents, but, on the other side of the Tasman Sea, the service is operated by the Australian Stamp Promotion Council which publishes personalised postcards with greetings from Santa. People wishing to have one of these cards sent to a child have to send a remittance to the Promotion Council's office in the local state capital. The cards are despatched with a special postmark on 6 December, St Nicholas Day. This scheme is used to raise money for children's charities.

Since 1981 the British Post Office has permitted local delivery of Christmas cards by Scout and Guide troops and Church groups, a condition of the service being that any profits accruing must be used for charitable purposes. Most of these services issue their own stamps which form a sideline to Christmas philately. Only two or three services of this kind operated in 1981 but the number rose substantially in 1982 and this looks like being an increasingly popular feature of Christmas from now on.

James Mackay

Christmas Coins

pecial coins for Christmas have only been minted in recent years, but they have an interesting precedent. In Victorian times a silver crown formed part of the coinage series and this large handsome coin, with its picture of St George and the Dragon on the reverse, was a popular birthday and Christmas gift from rich uncles to their nephews and nieces, at a time when it represented a quarter of the average weekly wage of an unskilled artisan. The crown was too large and cumbersome to be practical for everyday circulation, but its spending power (five shillings) for a youngster was enormous.

Crowns were on their way out by the end of the 19th century, and although they were included in the Coronation set honouring King Edward VII in 1902, they were not struck for general circulation. By 1911 they had become such a thing of the past that they were not even included in the proof set for the Coronation of King George V. Then, a quarter of a century after their last appearance, crowns were suddenly revived in 1927. This was due to the persistence of a band of leading numismatists who urged the Royal Mint to issue them specifically for the Christmas season. The Mint relented and in November, 1927, produced a proof version of a crown bearing the effigy of King George V on the obverse and an entirely new reverse showing a Tudor crown surrounded by a garland of the heraldic flowers of the United Kingdom. Some 15 030 proofs were sold and largely distributed as Christmas presents. Considering its relatively low mintage this is a sadly neglected coin, with a present-day value around £100.

The Tudor crown design by Kruger Gray was used for subsequent Christmas crowns until 1936, with the exception of 1935 when a special crown commemorating the Silver Jubilee of King George V was issued instead. Demand for these comparatively expensive stocking-fillers fell sharply after the initial furore to an average of 4000–5000 each December, but in the gloomy year of 1932, in the depths of the Depression, demand sank to a mere 2395. It rose again in 1933 to over 7000 but only 932 were sold in 1934, making this one of the rarest British coins of this century. Only 2473 were issued in 1936. The crowns of 1928–36 were intended for general circulation and were legal tender, though the majority were probably preserved by collectors. No Christmas crowns were issued after that time, and these handsome large-sized coins were later confined to Coronation sets (1937 and 1953) and occasional commemoration of special events.

The idea of a special coin at Christmas, with a different motif each year, began in the Isle of Man as recently as 1979. The Isle of Man has issued its own coins intermittently for the past three centuries and has regularly issued its own coins since 1970. In 1978 it introduced a circulating £1 coin, in the traditional sovereign size but struck in a base metal alloy called virenium. The reverse of this coin showed the triskelion or three-legged emblem superimposed on a map of the island. A special edition of this coin was struck in 1979 and mounted in greetings folders for use as Christmas presents. The special coins were distinguished from the ordinary circulating version by the inclusion of a tiny privy mark

Isle of Man 50p coin depicting Douglas Harbour in 1830

below the map on the reverse, in the form of a snow crystal. The success of the Christmas pound encouraged the Isle of Man authorities to go a stage further and issue a coin with a distinctive design. It was decided to mint a special 50p coin as an inexpensive Christmas gift and the first coin in this series was launched in November, 1980. The obverse bears the Machin profile of Queen Elizabeth, and resembles the ordinary circulating 50p coins. But the reverse was headed CHRISTMAS and depicted a panoramic view of Douglas Harbour in 1830. This coin coincided with the 150th anniversary of the Isle of Man Steam Packet Company and, appropriately, showed the arrival of the paddle-steamer *Mona's Queen* with the Christmas mail from Liverpool. The coin was minted in cupro-nickel for general circulation, but collectors' versions were also released in sterling silver. An attractive feature of the latter was their availability mounted in special Christmas cards whose full-colour vignette reproduced the motif on the coin.

Since 1981 had been designated International Fishermen's Year the Christmas coin combined this theme with a reference to the Manx traditional custom of dressing the mast-head of fishing boats. The coin showed the departure of the fishing fleet from Peel in about 1850. In the centre of the picture was a Manx 'nickey', or inshore fishing-boat, with a Christmas garland at the masthead. This was connected with the ancient and rather barbaric custom known as Hunt the Wren, it being considered good luck to kill one of these tiny birds and place it in the centre of a basket interwoven with holly, ivy and evergreens. This was strapped to the mast on 26 December and was supposed to bring good luck to the fishermen for the ensuing year.

For the 1982 coin the subject was carol-singers around the giant Christmas tree in the main square at Castletown, with Castle Rushen in the background. This design had a Dickensian flavour, since the costume of the singers was mid-Victorian. By contrast, the 1983 coin moves forward to the 1920s and depicts the Christmas market in Ramsey. In the foreground can be seen a tailless Manx cat just escaping from the wheels of a motor-car whose occupants are bearing home an enormous Christmas tree. All of the Manx Christmas coins so far have been designed by Leslie Lindsay, who has created a series of delightful vignettes crammed with detail.

So far only one other country has followed this lead. In 1982 the Pacific kingdom of Tonga issued a one pa'anga coin in various editions – cupro-nickel, silver, gold and platinum – as a Christmas gift tailored to all pockets and purses. The obverse portrays King Taufa'ahau Tupou IV, while the reverse shows The Praying Hands, one of the best-loved engravings by Albrecht Dürer, surrounded by nine tiny Stars of Bethlehem.

The Manx and Tongan Christmas coins have all been struck by the Pobjoy Mint of Sutton, Surrey.

Reverse and obverse of the pa'anga coin

James Mackay

Christmas Stamps

Since stamp-collecting is a hobby associated with the long winter nights, it is appropriate that stamps are regularly issued to mark the Christmas season. Nowadays more than ninety countries issue such stamps, mainly to add a touch of colour to greetings cards and parcels, but in some cases bearing a small premium in aid of charities.

The first Christmas stamp appeared 85 years ago and came into this category almost by chance. The Canadian postal authorities reduced their Imperial postage rate from three to two cents in December, 1898, and to mark the occasion a commemorative stamp, designed by the Postmaster General, William Mulock, was released. It depicted a map of the world with the British Empire picked out in red, and bore the stirring legend 'We hold a vaster Empire than has been,' a quotation from the Song of Empire which Sir Lewis Morris composed in honour of the Golden Jubilee of Queen Victoria in 1887.

The story goes that the issue was originally planned for 9 November, the birthday of the Prince of Wales. It is said that when a postal official informed Queen Victoria that the stamp would also mark the Prince's birthday she asked jealously, 'Which Prince?' To which the official tactfully replied, 'Why, Madam – the Prince of Peace of course.' And so XMAS 1898 came to be inscribed on the stamp. Be that as it may, Imperial Penny Postage was, in fact, introduced on Christmas Day, 1898, and

the stamp was actually released on 7 December. It was a remarkable stamp in that it was printed in three colours involving two different printing processes. The Empire was coloured bright red and somewhat more was thus shaded than should have been at the time, for the whole of southern Africa was shown in that colour, though another four years were to elapse before this became a fact, with the annexation of the Orange Free State and the Transvaal at the end of the Boer War.

Apart from this one occasion no country issued special Christmas stamps for almost forty years. Then, in 1937, Austria produced a pair of stamps showing a nosegay of roses flanked by the signs of the zodiac. A curious 'ghost portrait' appeared in this design: one of the roses in the vase bore an uncanny resemblance to Adolf Hitler, moustache and all. This was regarded as a bad omen at the time, and was subsequently justified by events, for Nazi troops invaded Austria the following March and proclaimed the *Anschluss*, or union with Germany. The Christmas stamps were, in fact, the last issue of the independent Austrian Republic until the country was liberated in 1945. Austria did not resume the issue of Christmas stamps until 1948, when a 60 groschen stamp was produced to mark the 130th anniversary of the carol *Silent Night*. Father Joseph Mohr and his organist, Franz Grüber, who composed this much-loved carol on Christmas Eve 1818, were portrayed on the stamp. Stamps showing a little girl gazing up at a Christmas tree were issued in 1953 and 1954, while Josef Stammel's painting of the Holy Family was reproduced on a Christmas stamp in 1963, but it was not until 1967 that Christmas stamps were issued regularly by Austria.

Neighbouring Hungary issued a set of three stamps in 1943, when the Second World War was at its height. The stamps depicted the Shepherds and Angels (4 filler), the Nativity (20f) and the Adoration of the Wise Men (30f). This proved to be an isolated case, however, and Hungary has never issued any Christmas stamps since then.

The Austrian and Hungarian stamps were issued without a charity premium and were intended for use on greetings cards. In some other countries, however, it had long been the custom to issue stamps with a charity surcharge in aid of orphans, the poor, the aged and the infirm. For many years such countries as Belgium, the Netherlands, Luxembourg, France, Germany and Switzerland had issued these charity stamps around the Christmas period, and continue to do so to this day. In Latin America this practice was followed to a lesser extent. In some cases the use of charity stamps was compulsory on greetings correspondence and by this means Cuba raised money for its anti-TB campaign from 1939 onwards. In 1951 these compulsory charity stamps were joined by 1 and 2 centavo stamps depicting Christmas emblems and inscribed NAVIDADES, the Spanish equivalent of Christmas. A Christmas tree was depicted in 1952, while Santa Claus was portrayed in 1954. Subsequently a turkey (1955), the Three Wise Men (1956) and the Nativity (1957) were featured, but thereafter the Cuban Christmas stamps took on a more secular and thematic character, showing flowers, birds, butterflies, reptiles and other

fauna. In 1960 the Christmas issue took the form of a sheet of 25 stamps with different designs, showing various flowers. Sixteen of the stamps were arranged in groups of four, surrounded by an oval border on which was inscribed the words and music of a Christmas hymn.

Costa Rica was another early exponent of Christmas stamps which also evolved out of an obligatory tax to raise money for charity. In 1958 two stamps were issued with a 5 centavo surcharge in aid of the Juvenile Delinquents' Fund, which promoted the establishment of a children's village on the same lines as the famous Boys' Town in Nebraska, USA. These stamps were inscribed SELLO DE NAVIDAD (Christmas stamp) and their use was compulsory on greetings cards. Father Flanagan, founder of Boys' Town, was portrayed on the 1959 stamps.

In 1957, however, Australia became the first Commonwealth country to issue stamps without a charity surcharge, for use on greetings cards. Two stamps were released, showing the Star of Bethlehem and a child at prayer, based on the painting entitled *The Child Samuel* by Sir Joshua Reynolds in the National Gallery, London. For a number of years Australia's Christmas stamps emphasised the religious aspect of this great festival. In 1958 the Nativity and in 1959 the approach of the Magi to Bethlehem, were depicted. The 350th anniversary of the English translation of the Bible, authorised by King James I in 1611, was alluded to in the Christmas stamps of 1960 and 1961, featuring a Bible and a richly illuminated book of hours inscribed with appropriate Christmas texts. In the latter year Australia's dependency, Norfolk Island, began issuing Christmas stamps in the same design, and this practice continued till 1966 when Norfolk Island introduced its own distinctive motifs.

The idea of issuing Christmas stamps was slow to catch on. Spain issued an 80 centimo stamp in 1955, reproducing El Greco's painting of the Holy Family. This is a very scarce stamp nowadays in mint condition, and relatively few were sold at the time. This deterred the Spanish postal authorities from repeating the experiment until 1959, but since then stamps inscribed NAVIDAD and usually reproducing sacred works of art have appeared each December.

Thanks to the lead given by Australia, Christmas stamps enjoyed their widest popularity in the Pacific area. New Zealand began issuing Christmas stamps in 1960. The first stamp depicted the rather sombre *Adoration of the Shepherds*, after Rembrandt, which hangs in the National Gallery, London. The scene in the stable is painted in hues of deepest brown, relief being provided only by the reddish glow from the lantern held by one of the shepherds. In the printing process the red colour was inadvertently omitted from a few of these stamps, and the 'Black Christmas', as the error was promptly dubbed by collectors, is now listed in the Gibbons catalogue at £300. In subsequent years till 1969 New Zealand issued a single stamp, usually reproducing an Old Master painting in full colour. The sole exception to this was the stamp issued in 1964, which showed the Rev Samuel Marsden preaching the first Christmas sermon in New Zealand 150 years earlier. Since 1969 New Zealand has invariably issued three stamps each year, featuring some aspect of a local church, reproducing a religious painting, and showing a secular subject associated with the season. In this way both the strictly religious and the purely festive nature of Christmas are covered. From 1967 till 1972 the New Zealand dependency of Niue had Christmas stamps in the same design as the mother country, and in 1969 -70 the Tokelau Islands did likewise. Subsequently Niue adopted local designs. The neighbouring Cook Islands became an enthusiastic issuer of Christmas stamps in 1967 and has since explored every aspect of religious art relevant to the Nativity. Furthermore, its dependencies of Aitutaki and Penrhyn have also issued their own lengthy Christmas sets since 1972 and 1973 respectively, in the same genre.

In 1964 Christmas stamps spread to other parts of the Commonwealth. Canada, whose 1898 issue can only be regarded as accidental, introduced bona fide Christmas stamps in October, 1964, the two stamps showing a typical family looking up at the Nativity Star. Malawi became the first country in Africa to issue such stamps, a set of four showing the Nativity Star above the globe. Malta issued three stamps designed by Chevalier Cremona and showing his interpretation of the Nativity.

The following year Britain issued two special air letter sheets or aerogrammes, with impressed stamps featuring snowflakes and two different pictorial designs on the reverse of the sheets showing the Adoration of the Shepherds and a Christmas tree with ice crystals respectively. Since then Christmas air letter sheets have been a regular feature of the British issue, but adhesive stamps were not introduced till 1966.

Britain's first stamps on this theme were produced as the result of a children's design competition. More than 5000 children under 16 took part and eventually prizes were awarded to two 6-year-olds, Tasveer Shemza and James Berry, whose designs were used for 3d and 1s 6d stamps. The pictorial design on the accompanying First Day envelope was by the runner-up, 9-year-old Ann Belshaw. In later years Britain preferred the work of adult professional designers, but returned to the original concept for the stamps of 1981. On this occasion the 11½p stamp was designed by 5½-year-old Samantha Brown, who thus became the world's youngest stamp designer. Over the years since 1967 Britain has shown a marked preference for religious subjects. Some sets were derived from religious works of art, such as Old Master paintings (1967), the De Lisle Psalter (1970), stained glass windows (1971), medieval painted church roof bosses (1974) and medieval ecclesiastical embroidery (1976). Christmas carols have also been used, notably in the set of 1973 which told the story of Good King Wenceslas in a strip of five 3p stamps, and the issue of 1977 which used the same technique to depict all the objects enumerated in 'The Twelve Days of Christmas'. In other years symbolism associated with the Christmas festival has been used. In 1968 alone was the more materialistic aspect of Christmas depicted, when three stamps by Rosalind Dease showed middle-class children playing with expensive new toys; this provoked such a storm of protest that the Post Office has

CHRISTMAS
GREETINGS

16.11.83

St·MARY-LE-STRAND
LONDON W.C.2.

sensibly avoided the topic ever since.

The United States began issuing Christmas stamps in 1962, a single 4 cent stamp showing a Christmas wreath. This seemed innocuous enough, but the issue of a stamp devoted to Christianity was sufficient to rouse the ire of non-Christian communities who argued that such action was unconstitutional. The USPO wisely ignored such carping criticism and persevered in issuing Christmas stamps in subsequent years, although there was a tendency to play down the religious aspects by depicting a Christmas tree (1963) and Christmas flowers in a block of four (1964). By 1965 opposition to Christmas stamps had receded sufficiently for the USPO to issue a stamp showing a weather vane in the form of the Archangel Gabriel. Significantly the only criticism on that occasion was the age-old controversy over whether angels, who are supposedly asexual, should be depicted with breasts. After that the USPO went boldly for old master paintings, backed by the growing body of opinion that Christmas stamps should have a more religious flavour. Since 1971, however, the USPO has issued at least two stamps each year, one sacred and the other secular in its approach.

The Christmas stamps of 1975 were unusual in that no value was expressed on them. This was due to the fact that, at the time the stamps were being printed, an increase in postal rates seemed imminent, but the amount of the increase had not been settled.

In the same year that Spain began issuing Christmas stamps regularly – 1959 – the

Vatican followed suit. Not surprisingly, the Vatican stamps have drawn on the vast art repository of the Catholic church for their inspiration. This idea was slow to catch on elsewhere. San Marino did not adopt Christmas stamps till 1967 and abandoned them in 1969, not reviving an annual issue till 1973. Italy's first Christmas stamp, inscribed NATALE, appeared in 1974. Among the countries of northern Europe West Germany and West Berlin added Christmas stamps to their annual Welfare sets in 1969. Like the *Wohlfartsmarke*, which have a tradition going back to 1924, the German Christmas stamps have adopted a frankly thematic approach, though over the past decade the religious aspect has been gradually emphasised. Among the Scandinavian countries, Sweden was the first to issue Christmas stamps, in 1970. Finland followed in 1974 and Norway a year later, but in Scandinavia greater prominence is accorded to charity seals. Like France and Germany, Belgium has a long history of charity stamps around the Christmas season, but since 1970 a stamp has also been issued for use on greetings cards.

Christmas stamps have also spread gradually throughout Latin America. Considering the influence of Catholicism it is surprising that Christmas stamps have not made greater strides there. Venezuela has issued them regularly since 1965, but Nicaragua and Uruguay did not adopt them till 1972, Colombia a year later and Chile and Mexico only since 1977. Peru had a compulsory charity issue in 1968, and this was a prelude to regular Christmas stamps from 1969 onwards. Argentina has issued Christmas stamps since 1970 and ranged from

Old Masters to children's drawings. Undoubtedly the most interesting Christmas stamps from Latin America were the lengthy issues made by Nicaragua. The first set (of nine stamps) illustrated the legend of the Christmas rose, but the following year (1973) the nine stamps told the moving story of little Virginia O'Hanlon who wrote a letter to the American *Sun* newspaper asking 'Does Santa Claus exist?' Among the issues of later years, the set of 1975, featuring famous choirs of the world, was outstanding.

Undoubtedly the greatest impetus to Christmas philately has come from the British Commonwealth. In addition to the countries already mentioned, Gibraltar, Guyana and St Lucia began issuing such stamps in 1967, but the following year more than a dozen countries ranging from the West Indies to Polynesia joined in and the number has risen steadily ever since. In the British Isles, the Republic of Ireland has had Christmas stamps since 1971, while Guernsey, Jersey and the Isle of Man have all issued their own distinctive stamps.

Over the past decade alone the trend has been to escape from the well-tried themes of Old Master paintings. Other forms of religious art, from stained glass and embroidery to carved pews and roof bosses have also been explored, while both Greece and Cyprus have drawn on a seemingly endless supply of icons and frescoes for inspiration. In more recent years individual Christmas carols have become a popular subject, enabling the artist considerable scope. Christmas Island has, understandably, been one of the leading exponents of Christmas stamps, and in 1977–8 issued

sets of stamps in the form of miniature
sheets illustrating the words and music of
'The Twelve Days of Christmas' and 'The
Song of Christmas' respectively.

Inevitably, as postal administrations look
farther afield for suitable subjects, considerable ingenuity is being shown while
some motifs have stretched the bounds of
relevance to the limit. Among the odd
subjects chosen for Christmas stamps may
be mentioned Millie, the talking (and
swearing) parrot who was such a hit at the
Montreal Expo '67 and who graced the
Christmas stamps of Guyana in 1967 and
1968. The stamps from the Crown dependencies of the British Isles have provided
a high proportion of the quaint and the
unusual, from the Manx 5p of 1978 showing
the traditional custom called 'Hunt the
Wren' to Jersey's 18p of 1981 featuring the
Boxing Day meeting of the Jersey Drag
Hunt. Occasionally Christmas is linked to
other events, hence the large number of
stamps depicting the works of Michelan-

Christmas Carols 1982
ROYAL MAIL FIRST DAY COVER

gelo, Dürer, Rubens and other artists on the occasion of their centenaries. In 1982, however, the BBC celebrated the 50th anniversary of the first Christmas broadcast by King George V – an event that provided Ascension and Jersey with the themes for their Christmas issues that year.

Mention has been made of the special pictorial air letter sheets issued by Britain since 1965. Similar aerogrammes have been issued by Australia since 1961, while the New Zealand Post Office sells unstamped greetings aerogrammes of a pictorial character. Special Christmas greetings telegrams have been produced by several countries, while during the Second World War micro-filmed greetings, known in Britain as airgraphs and in America as V-mail, were sent by servicemen all over the world between 1941 and 1944.

In 1978 the British Post Office launched its first Christmas booklet of stamps. Each booklet contained strips of the prevailing first and second class postage stamps side

British Philatelic Bureau
20 Brandon Street
EDINBURGH
EH3 5TT

Royal Mail First Day Cover

by side while the cover had an attractive Christmas motif. It was intended that these booklets would make an ideal and inexpensive gift from children to their Old Age Pensioner grandparents. This idea was repeated in subsequent years, but was taken a step farther in 1982 when booklets containing stamps worth £2.80 were sold at a discount of 30p. To prevent the discount stamps being detached and sold at the full price each stamp was issued with a blue Star of Bethlehem printed on the reverse, beneath the gum. As before, the booklet cover had an appropriate Christmas motif, but the stamps themselves (12½p and 15½p definitives) thus became distinctive and merit inclusion in any collection of Christmas stamps.

James Mackay

VI

Abroad

WELCOME TO
CHRISTMAS ISLAND

Places with a Christmas Flavour

Fred Jurgen Specovius, the world's most travelled man. Christmas Island was just one of the stopping points on his schedule which took in 170 sovereign countries. (See also previous page.)

A number of places which were either discovered or founded on Christmas Day are named appropriately. The South African province of Natal was discovered by Vasco da Gama on Christmas Day, 1497, and takes its name from the Portuguese word for Christmas. From 1857 until 1910 Natal had its own stamps but no longer features in the list of stamp-issuing countries; its place has been taken by Christmas Island.

Actually, there are three places of that name – one in Canada and two in the Southern Hemisphere. Both of the latter have, or had, their own stamps. Christmas Island in the Central Pacific had its own distinctive stamps from 1915 till 1936, issued by the Central Pacific Cocoanut Plantations Ltd, which leased the island. From 1942 until 1948 the island was an American army base and in the 1950s it was used by Britain for nuclear tests and British stamps on mail from military and scientific personnel bore a distinctive Christmas Island postmark. It now forms part of the nation of Kiribati – pronounced kiri-bass – which comprises 33 ocean specks straddling the International Date Line, 264 square miles of land scattered over two million square miles of the Pacific. It has four settlements, quaintly named London, Paris, Poland and Banana.

Christmas Island in the eastern Indian Ocean, south of Java, was once administered by Singapore but was transferred to Australia in 1958 and has since had its own stamps. It was discovered by William Dampier on Christmas Day, 1688, but not colonised till 1889. It was occupied by the Japanese in the Second World War but liberated by Australian forces in 1945. Although it has a conservative stamp-issuing policy, Christmas Island has produced some of the most colourful and interesting Christmas stamps of recent years.

Fort Christmas in Florida was founded in 1835 and a post office, named simply Christmas, was opened in 1892. In recent years it has handled upwards of 300 000 items each December, both handstruck and machine cancellations being accompanied by a cachet depicting a Christmas tree and the slogan 'Glory to God in the Highest'. Special Christmas postmarks are also provided at Christmas, Missouri, while among the other American postmarks sought at this season of the year are those used at Christmas Cove (Maine) and Christmas Valley (Oregon).

The hamlet of Christmas Hills in Tasmania does not normally boast a postal facility, but, as a special dispensation at Christmas, the Australian Post Office provided a pictorial canceller in 1982 inscribed 'Christmas Greetings from Santa Claus'. Santa Claus himself has given his name to villages in California and Indiana and both of these have had special postmarks and cachets applied to greetings correspondence. The town of Santa Claus, Indiana, celebrated its centenary in 1952 with a slogan postmark showing the rubicund gentleman himself.

The city of Natal in Brazil, founded on Christmas Day, 1597, as a fortress to stamp out mahogany smuggling, is now the capital

Three postmen at Bethlehem. This one
is near Llandelio, Wales

of the state of Rio Grande do Norte but it
still remembers its origin each December,
with a special postmark showing the Infant
Jesus.

The village of Christkindl in Austria liter-
ally means 'little Christ child'. It was not
important enough to have a permanent post
office but in 1950 a temporary facility was
opened at the village inn and a pictorial
postmark showing the Christ child was
applied on mail sent from all over the world.
Since 1954, however, a different motif has
been used each year and Christkindl has
grown in importance. A stamp showing the
village church was added to the Austrian

definitive series in 1958, the year that the Christkindl postmark showed the opening bars of 'Silent Night' to celebrate the 140th anniversary of the famous carol.

A special Christmas postmark is provided each year for use on mail posted in the hamlet of Bethlehem near Llandeilo in Wales. Similar Christmas mailings occur from the places called Bethlehem in New Zealand and South Africa, as well as the Bethlehems in Georgia, Indiana, Kentucky and Maryland. As if this were not enough, the postmarks from Holly (Michigan), Mistletoe (Kentucky) and Snowflake (Arizona) are also much-prized on seasonal greetings cards.

James Mackay

Christmas at Sea – I

The sheets were frozen
hard, and they cut the
naked hand;
The decks were like a
slide, where a seaman
scarce could stand;
The wind was a nor'-
wester, blowing squally
off the sea;
And cliffs and spouting
breakers were the only
things a-lee.

They heard the surf a-
roaring before the break
of day;

But 'twas only with the peep of light we saw how ill we lay.
We tumbled every hand on deck instanter, with a shout,
And we gave her the maintops'l, and stood by to go about.

All day we tacked and tacked between the South Head and the North;
All day we hauled the frozen sheets, and got no further forth;
All day as cold as charity, in bitter pain and dread,
For very life and nature we tacked from head to head.

We gave the South a wider berth, for there the tide-race roared;
But every tack we made we brought the North Head close aboard:
So's we saw the cliffs and houses, and the breakers running high,
And the coastguard in his garden, with his glass against his eye.

The frost was on the village roofs as white as ocean foam;
The good red fires were burning bright in every 'long-shore home;
The windows sparkled clear, and the chimneys volleyed out;
And I vow we sniffed the victuals as the vessel went about.

The bells upon the church were rung with a mighty jovial cheer;
For it's just that I should tell you how (of all days in the year)

This day of our adversity was blessed Christmas morn,
And the house above the coastguard's was the house where I was born.

O well I saw the pleasant room, the pleasant faces there,
My mother's silver spectacles, my father's silver hair;
And well I saw the firelight, like a flight of homely elves,
Go dancing round the china-plates that stand upon the shelves.

And well I knew the talk they had, the talk that was of me,
Of the shadow on the household and the son that went to sea;
And O the wicked fool I seemed, in every kind of way,
To be here and hauling frozen ropes on blessed Christmas Day.

They lit the high sea-light, and the dark began to fall.
'All hands to loose topgallant sails,' I heard the captain call.
'By the Lord, she'll never stand it,' our first mate, Jackson, cried.
. . . 'It's the one way or the other, Mr Jackson,' he replied.

She staggered to her bearings, but the sails were new and good,
And the ship smelt up to windward just as though she understood,
As the winter's day was ending, in the entry of the night,
We cleared the weary headland, and passed below the light.

And they heaved a mighty breath, every soul on board but me,
As they saw her nose again pointing handsome out to sea;
But all that I could think of, in the darkness and the cold,
Was just that I was leaving home and my folks were growing old.

Robert Louis Stevenson

Christmas at Sea – II

From the Diary of the Reverend Henry Teonge, Naval Chaplain.

Henry Teonge (1621–1690) went to sea as chaplain on board the *Assistance* in 1675 and later served aboard the *Bristol* and the *Royal Oak*. His diary, which shows him to have been a pleasant, easy-going man, gives an amusing picture of life in the navy at that time.

1675

Christmas Day we keepe thus: At four in the morning our trumpeters all do flat their trumpets, and begin at our Captain's cabin, and thence to all the officers' and gentlemen's cabins; playing a levite* at each cabin door, and bidding good morrow, wishing a merry Christmas. After they go to their station, viz on the poop, and sound three levites in honour of the morning. At ten we go to prayers and sermon; text Zacc. ix:9. Our Captain had all his officers and gentlemen to dinner with him where we had excellent good fare: a rib of beef, plum-puddings, mince pies, &c., and plenty of good wines of several sorts; drank healths to the King, to our wives and friends, and ended the day with much civil mirth.

1678

Good Christmas Day. We go to prayers at 10; and the wind rose of such a sudden that I was forced (by the Captain's command) to conclude abruptly at the end of the Litany; and we had no sermon . . . We had not so great a dinner as was intended, for, the whole fleet being in this harbour, beef

* Usually *levet*: a trumpet call or musical train to rouse soldiers or others in the morning *OED*

'Trumpeters all do flat their trumpets'

could not be got. Yet we had a dinner of an excellent rice pudding in a great charger, a special piece of Martinmas English beef, and a neat's* tongue, and a good cabbage, a charger full of excellent fresh fish fried, a dozen of woodcocks in a pie, which cost 15d., a couple of good hens roasted, three sorts of cheese, and, last of all, a great charger full of blue figs, almonds, and raisins; wine and punch galore, and a dozen of English pippins.

* An animal of the ox-kind; an ox or bullock; a cow or heifer. Now *rare OED*

Christmas Day in the Army

T he following account of Christmas Day in a Cavalry Regiment was written in 1875 by Archibald Forbes, then a well-known journalist, who had served in the Royal Dragoons between 1859 and 1864:

Christmas Day is the great regimental merry-making . . . About a month before, self-deniant fellows busy themselves in constructing 'dimmocking bags' for the occasion, such being the barrack-room term for receptacles for money-hoarding purposes. The weak vessels manage to cheat their fragility of 'saving grace' by requesting their sergeant-major to put them 'on the peg' – that is to say, place them under stoppages . . . Everybody becomes of a sudden astonishingly sober and steady . . . The guardroom is unwontedly empty – nobody except the utterly reckless will get into trouble just now . . .

The clever hands of the troop are deep in devising a series of ornamentations for the walls and roof of the common habitation. One fellow spends all his spare time . . . embellishing the wall above the fireplace with a florid design in a variety of colours meant to be an exact copy of the device on the regiment's kettledrums, with the addition of the legend 'A Merry Christmas to the Old Strawboots', inscribed on a waving scroll below. The skill of another decorator is directed to the clipping of sundry squares of coloured paper into wondrous forms – Prince of Wales's feathers, gorgeous festoons, and the like – with which the gas pendants and the edges of the window-frames are disguised . . .

A couple of days before 'the day', the sergeant-major enters the barrack-room . . . He cannot refrain from the customary short patronising harangue, 'Our worthy captain – liberal gent you know – deputed me – what you like for dinner – plum-puddings of course – a quart of beer a man; make up your minds what you'll have – anything but game and venison'; and so he vanishes grinning a saturnine grin . . . The alternative lies between pork and goose . . . Goose versus pork is eagerly debated. As regards quantity the question is a level one, since the allowance from time immemorial has been a goose or a leg of pork among three men . . . The sergeant-major is informed of the conclusion arrived at (after the evening stables), and the corporal of each room accompanies him on a marketing expedition into town (taking with him the contents of the 'dimmocking bags' and the stoppages in the sergeant-major's hands) . . . He goes direct to the fountain-head. If there is a brewery in the place he finds it out and bestows his order upon it, thus triumphantly securing the pure article at the wholesale price. His purchasing calculation is upon the basis of two gallons per man. (For twelve men) he orders a twenty-four gallon barrel of porter – always porter (a dark brown bitter beer, brewed from partly charred malt) . . .

It is Christmas Eve. The evening stable-hour is over and all hands are merrily engaged in the composition of the puddings; some stoning fruit, others chopping suet, beating egg and so forth . . . (Usually one man is the acknowledged pudding-maker expert). His comrades pull out their clean towels for pudding-cloths; they run to the canteen enthusiastically for a further supply on a hint from him that there is a deficiency in the ingredient of allspice. And then he artistically gathers together the corners of the cloths and ties up the puddings tightly and securely; whereupon a procession is formed to escort them to the cook-house, and there, having consigned them into the depths of the mighty copper, the 'man of the time' remains watching the cauldron bubble until morning, a great jorum of beer at his elbow, the ready contribution of his appreciative comrades . . .

(Christmas Day.) On an ordinary morning the reveille is practically negatived, and nobody thinks of stirring from between the blankets till the 'warning' sounds a quarter of an hour before the morning stabletime. But on this morning there is no slothful skulking . . . The soldier's wife who has the cleaning of the room and who does the washing for its inmates – for which services each man pays her a penny a day, has from time immemorial taken upon herself the duty of bestowing a 'morning' on the Christmas anniversary upon the men she 'does for'. Accordingly, about a quarter to six she enters the room . . . She carries a bottle of whisky – it is always whisky, somehow – in one hand and a glass in the other; and, beginning with the oldest soldier administers a calker (a dram) to every one in the room till she comes to the 'cruity', upon whom, if he is a pullet-faced, homesick, bit of a lad, she may bestow a maternal salute in addition, with the advice to consider the regiment as his mother now . . .

(Church parade follows morning stables) but there are two of the inmates of each room who do not go to church. The clever pudding-maker and a sub of his selection are left to cook the Christmas dinner. This, as regards the exceptional dainties, is done at the barrack-room fire, the cook-house being in use only for the now despised ration meat and for the still simmering puddings. The handy man cunningly improvises a roasting-jack, and erects a screen consisting of bed-quilts spread on a frame of upright forms, for the purpose of retaining and throwing back the heat . . .

There is a large expanse of table in every barrack-room . . . Bare boards at a Christmas feast are horribly offensive to the eye of taste. Something must be done; something has already been done. Ever since the last issue of clean sheets (which took place once a month), one or two whole-souled fellows have magnanimously abjured these luxuries pro bono publico. Spartan-like they have lain in blankets, and saved their sheets in their pristine cleanliness wherewithal to cover the Christmas table . . .

(After church parade and watering and feeding the horses the men) assemble fully dressed in the barrack-room, hungrily silent. The captain enters the room and pro forma asks whether there are 'any complaints'. A chorus of 'No, sir' is his reply; and then the oldest soldier in the room with profuse blushing and stammering takes up the running, thanks the officer kindly in the name of his comrades for his generosity, and wishes him a 'Happy Christmas and many of 'em' in return. Under cover of the responsive cheer the captain makes his escape, and a deputation visits the sergeant-major's quarters to fetch the allowance of beer which forms part of the treat. Then they fall to and eat! Ye gods, how they eat! (In twenty minutes of silent eating) be the fare goose or pork, it is, barring the bones, only 'a memory of the past'. The puddings, turned out of the towels in which they have been boiled, then undergo the brunt of a fierce assault; but the edge of appetite has been blunted by the first course and with most of the men a modicum of pudding goes on the shelf for supper.

At length dinner is over. Beds are drawn up from the sides of the room so as to form a wide circle of divans round the fire, and the big barrel's time has come at last. A clever hand whips out the bung, draws a pailful, and reinserts the bung till another pailful is wanted which will be very soon. The pail is placed upon the hearthstone and its contents are decanted into the pint basins, which do duty in the barrack-room for all purposes from containing coffee and soup to mixing chrome-yellow and pipe-clay water. The married soldiers come dropping in with their wives, for whom the corporal has a special drop of 'something short' stowed away in reserve on the shelf behind his kit. A song is called for ... The songs of soldiers are never of the modern music-hall type. You never hear such a ditty as 'Champagne Charley' or 'Not for Joseph'. The soldier takes especial delight in songs of the sentimental pattern; and even when he forsakes the region of sentiment, it is to give vent to such sturdy bacchanalian out-pourings as the 'Good Rhine Wine', 'Old John Barleycorn' and 'Simon the Cellarer'. But these are only interludes. 'The Soldier's Tear', 'The White Squall', 'There came a Tale of England', 'Ben Bolt', 'Shells of the Ocean' and other melodies of a lugubrious type, are the special favourites of the barrack-room ...

Songs and beer form the staple of the afternoon's enjoyment ... There is no speechifying ...

It is a lucky thing for a good many that there is no roll-call at the Christmas evening stable-hour. The non-commissioned officers mercifully limit their requirements to seeing the horses watered and bedded down by the most presentable of the roisterers ... This interruption over, the circle re-forms round the fire, and the cask finally becomes a 'dead marine'.

'A song is called for'

A Gift from the Legion

When I was a boy, which was a good many years ago, there was a very queer celebration on New Year's Day in the little Monmouthshire town where I was born, Caerleon-on-Usk. The town children – village children would be nearer the mark, since the population of the place amounted to a thousand souls or thereabouts – got the biggest and bravest and gayest apple they could find in the loft, deep in the dry bracken. They put bits of gold leaf upon it. They stuck raisins into it. They inserted into the apple little sprigs of box, and then they delicately slit the ends of hazel-nuts, and so worked that the nuts appeared to grow from the ends of the box leaves, to be disproportionate fruit of these small trees. At last, three bits of stick were fixed into the base of the apple, tripod-wise, and so it was borne round from house to house; and the children got cakes and sweets, and – those were wild days, remember – small cups of ale. And nobody knew what it was all about.

And here is the strangeness of it. Caerleon means the Fort of the Legions, and for about three hundred years the Second Augustan Legion was quartered there and made a tiny Rome of the place, with amphitheatre, baths, temples, and everything necessary for the comfort of a Roman-Briton. And the Legion brought over the custom of the *strena* (French, *étrennes*), the New Year's Gift of good omen. The apple, with its gold leaf, raisins, and nuts, meant 'good crops and wealth in the New Year'. It is the poet Martial, I think, who alludes to the custom. He was an ungrateful fellow; somebody sent him a gold cup as a New Year's gift, and he said the gold of the cup was so thin that it would have done very well to put on the festive apple of the day.

Well, I suppose the Second Augustan was recalled somewhere about AD 400. The Saxon came to Caerleon, and after him the Dane, and then the Norman, and then the modern spirit, the worst enemy of all; and still, up to fifty years ago, the Caerleon children kept New Year's Day as if the Legionaries were yet in garrison.

Arthur Machen

' . . . and so it was borne round from house to house.'

' . . . as if the Legionaries were yet in garrison.'

Christmas in Spain, 1824

T he Christmas festival is still observed in Madrid in the same manner that was practised a century ago. The evening of the vigil is scarcely dark when numbers of men, women, and boys are seen traversing the streets with torches, and many of them supplied with tambourines, which they strike loudly as they move along in a kind of Bacchanal procession. There is a tradition here that the shepherds who visited Bethlehem on the day of the Nativity had instruments of this sort upon which they expressed the sentiment of joy that animated them, when they received the intelligence that a SAVIOUR was born. Hence for weeks before Christmas there is a fair in Madrid, where scarcely anything but tambourines are sold, and every family, of the lower order at least, thinks it necessary to have one. If the younger branches do not issue into the streets with them, they use them in their houses; in some instances, aided by the guitar, they spend the whole night dancing to these tambourines, or to another instrument which they call a zambomba.*

At twelve o'clock, the midnight mass is celebrated in all the churches. As soon as the clock strikes, the priests come forth vested from the sacristy, and repair to the altar, which is already lighted and prepared for the occasion. The organ peals forth a hymn of joy, and the mass is commenced. During the service several pieces of national music are performed, particularly that which is called the Munnira, which is a fine old composition. But what is most remarkable in this ceremony is that crowds of people who, perhaps, had been traversing the streets the whole night, come into the church with their tambourines and guitars, and accompny the organ. I do not say that this is a custom deserving of approbation; to a foreigner, however, it appears a striking peculiarity, and when he considers it as a relic of old customs, he finds it the source of many strange and interesting reflections. When the mass is over, the musical groups begin to dance in the very body of the church, and there

---

* The zambomba is a very noisy instrument. A skin of moistened parchment is tied on the mouth of an earthen vase; and to the centre of the parchment is fixed a reed, by the friction of which, when the parchment is dry, a sound like that of the tambourine, when rubbed by the finger, is produced.

'. . . aided by the guitar'

is really so much of the spirit of joy in their motions, that though they are undoubtedly indecorous in this place, they are almost contagious. The fact is that there is a little of the spirit of the grape too in these scenes. The eve of Christmas-day is a strict fast, but the Spaniards, who very rarely drink much, indulge liberally on this occasion in wine; and though there are few of them actually intoxicated, they are generally a little elevated. The best consequence of the whole is that every body without exception is in a humour to please and to be pleased, an honourable trait in the national character, since it is well understood that the true disposition of the man appears unequivocally in his cups. You may say what you like to a Spaniard on this night, and he will not take offence. Everybody wears a smile on his countenance.

from A Visit to Spain by *M J Quin, 1824*

VII

Sport

Soccer at Christmas

Oldham Athletic were involved in two Boxing Day matches which produced different individual scoring records in two divisions. On 26 December 1935 Bunny Bell scored nine goals for Tranmere Rovers against Oldham in a Division Three (Northern) game but missed a second half penalty kick in Rovers, 13-4 win. Then 27 years later Oldham centre-forward Bert Lister scored six times for them when they beat Southport 11-0 in Division Four, which was also Oldham's record win.

The last occasion that a Division One match produced double figures for one side was on Boxing Day 1963 at Craven Cottage when Fulham beat Ipswich Town 10-1. It was Fulham's record win and Ipswich's heaviest defeat. Graham Leggat scored three goals in 3 minutes, the fastest hat-trick in Division One history. On the same day in another Division One game Blackburn Rovers won 8-2 at Upton Park against West Ham United. It was United's heaviest defeat on a day when 157 goals were scored in 39 League games, 66 of them coming from ten Division One matches. Two days later Ipswich beat Fulham 4-2 and West Ham won 3-1 at Blackburn.

Fulham's Graham Leggat, who made Division One history on Boxing Day 1963

Coventry City's Christmas present to their supporters on 25 December 1919 was to win 3-2 at Stoke City in a Division Two match during their first season in the Football League. It came after a run of 11 matches without a goal.

Three Sheffield Wednesday players, Norman Curtis, Eddie Gannon and Vince Kenny, each put through their own goal against West Bromwich Albion in a Division One match on Boxing Day 1952. Wednesday lost 5-4.

But on Christmas Day 1954 there was a heavier reverse for Rochdale against Carlisle United when Henry Boyle, Danny Murphy and George Underwood emulated this unusual 'hat-trick' by putting through their own goal in Rochdale's 7-2 defeat.

The fastest dismissal in Football League history occurred on Christmas Day 1936 at Hull when Wrexham's Scottish-born inside-right Ambrose Brown was sent off after 20 seconds of the start of a Division Three (Northern) match. Hull won 1-0.

Kevin Tully was sent off the field after making his debut for Blackpool at Burnley on 27 December 1971 in a Divison Two game. Burnley won 2-1.

Frank Swift made his debut in goal for Manchester City on Christmas Day 1933, the day after his 19th birthday. He then played in 234 out of City's next 235 League games up to the outbreak of the Second World War in 1939. The run included 192 consecutive appearances.

The first Football League game played on Christmas Day was on 25 December 1889 when Preston North End, the reigning champions, beat Aston Villa 3-2. The last two Football League games scheduled for a Christmas Day were in 1959.

Although several Football League clubs played two games on Christmas Day 1940

The highest aggregate of Football League attendances on one day occurred on Boxing Day 1949 when 1 253 570 watched a full programme of 44 matches in the four divisions.

The highest attendance to watch Manchester United at Old Trafford was 70 504 on 27 December 1920 in a Division One match against Aston Villa who won 3-1.

in North and South Regional League matches, Tommy Lawton and Len Shackleton each played for two different sides. In the morning Lawton led the Everton attack at Liverpool when they were beaten 3-1 and in the afternoon guested for Tranmere at home to Crewe Alexandra, scoring both Rovers' goals in a 2-2 draw. Shackleton played for the Bradford (Park Avenue) team beaten 2-1 at Leeds United in the morning, then guested for Bradford City in the afternoon heading a goal from 15 yards in City's 4-3 win at Huddersfield Town.

The peripatetic Len Shackleton, *above,* and Tommy Lawton, *right*

On the morning of 27 December 1948 Billy Gray played for Leyton Orient Reserves at Chelsea in the Football Combination and for the first team in Division Three (Southern) at home to Port Vale in the afternoon when Orient won 2-0.

Harry Lovatt played for Leicester City Reserves against Coventry City in the London Combination on Christmas Day 1930 and was then transferred to Notts County, playing for them against Coventry on 27 December in a Division Three (Southern) game. They won 4-1.

On Christmas Eve 1947 Harry Jackson, the Manchester City centre-forward, was transferred to Preston North End. On Christmas Eve 1948 he was transferred from Preston to Blackburn Rovers.

On 27 December 1930 Aston Villa defeated Manchester United 7-0 at Villa Park in a Division One match. United were relegated at the end of the season. On 26 December the following year United lost 7-0 away to Wolverhampton Wanderers in a Division Two game.

On Christmas Day 1952 Carlisle United beat Scunthorpe United 8-0 in a Division Three (Northern) match. It was Carlisle's record win and Scunthorpe's heaviest defeat.

On Christmas Day 1940 Brighton and Hove Albion travelled to Norwich City for a Regional League South match. They were only able to muster five players and their side was completed with City reserves and servicemen from the crowd. Norwich won 18-0 scoring in 3, 5, 15, 19, 23, 24, 29, 35, 40, 41, 52, 54, 69, 73, 75, 78, 80 and 83 minutes. Their half-time score of ten goals was the highest for one half in a wartime game.

On Christmas Day 1941 Bristol City set off for a match at Southampton in three cars. The last to leave contained centre-forward Clarrie Bourton and full-back Jack Preece together with the team's kit. This car arrived first but although the kick-off was delayed for an hour the other two cars did not appear.

Southampton manager Tom Parker offered to loan Bristol City five players plus their trainer Gallagher who had not played for several years. They completed a team with three spectators including a soldier and a schoolmaster.

Twenty minutes after the match started, the missing nine players arrived. One car had broken down and the other had stayed to assist, but it was too late to re-organise the City team so the substitutes played on while the nine sat in the stand and watched. Trainer Gallagher scored a goal against his old side but Southampton won 5-2.

Everton full-back Billy Cook scored penalties in three consecutive Division One matches within four days over Christmas 1938. On Saturday 24 December against Blackpool at Goodison Park, Everton won 4-0. Two days later at home to Derby County the match ended in a 2-2 draw while, on 27 December, Everton lost 2-1 at Derby. But Everton won the League championship that season.

On Boxing Day 1924 Nottingham Forest were awarded a penalty against Bolton Wanderers in a Division One match. At the time their regular penalty taker outside-left Harry Martin was in the dressing-room receiving attention from the trainer. Forest refused to take the kick until Martin was summoned from the treatment room and when he did appear on the field he scored from the spot kick to enable Forest to draw 1-1. Bolton protested after the match to no avail, but Forest finished bottom of the League and were relegated at the end of the season.

Walsall arrived at Barley Bank, Darwen on Boxing Day 1896 with seven players and a committee man whose registration was rushed through for the Division Two match. The rest of the team had missed their connection. With the aid of a strong wind after winning the toss and the clever disposition of their men, they managed to work the off-side trap, holding Darwen at bay for the first quarter of an hour. However, once they had broken through the home side quickly scored four goals and Walsall only crossed the half-way line three times in the first half. Despite heroic work by the Walsall goalkeeper after the interval, Darwen added a further eight to win 12-0.

Terry Butcher, England's centre-back was born on 28 December, 1958

Jack Rollin

Cricket at Christmas

Although Christmas marks the middle of cricket's hibernation period in Britain, interrupted by the occasional Boxing Day charity match on a matting pitch sometimes laid on snow, it is very much part of cricket overseas.

Three of the four Test cricketers born on Christmas Day began their lives in New Zealand: Clarrie Grimmett of Australia (born at Dunedin) in 1891, Donald McRae in 1912, Hedley Howarth – brother of the present New Zealand captain – in 1943, and Mansoor Akhtar of Pakistan in 1956. Two others were born on Boxing Day: Rohan Kanhai of West Indies in 1935, and the current Derbyshire captain, Barry Wood of England, in 1942. William Clarke, founder of both the All-England Eleven and the Trent Bridge Cricket Ground, was born in Nottingham on Christmas Eve in 1798.

Probably the most remarkable batting partnership of all began on Christmas morning in 1928 at the Melbourne Cricket Ground. Playing in Australia's national championship for the Sheffield Shield, visiting New South Wales had lost nine wickets for 113 runs in reply to Victoria's first innings total of 376 when their captain, Alan Kippax, was joined by the last batsman, Hal Hooker. Their stand continued well into Boxing Day. Nearly 25 hours had passed when John Edward Halford Hooker, an extremely accurate opening bowler who was unlucky never to gain selection at Test level, fell to a one-handed catch at mid-off. He had contributed 62 runs to a partnership of 307 which remains the world record for the tenth wicket in all first-class cricket. Kippax ('Mr Elegant') had taken his score from 22 to 260 not out as his team achieved a highly improbable lead of 44 runs. New South Wales went on to win the Sheffield Shield.

Two years earlier this same fixture between the main protagonists of Australian cricket had produced the world record total for all first-class matches when Victoria amassed 1107 on 27–28 December. Bill Ponsford (352) and Jack Ryder (295) were the main contributors to an innings which lasted only 10½ hours.

Christmas week of 1981 saw two world Test cricket records eclipsed. At Delhi on 23 December, Geoffrey Boycott overtook the record aggregate of 8032 runs by Sir Garfield Sobers. Four days later in Melbourne, Dennis Lillee broke Lance Gibbs's bowling record of 309 wickets.

The first women's Test match was played

World test records were broken in 1981 by Dennis Lillee (Australia), *above*, and Geoffrey Boycott (England), *right*

between Australia and England at Brisbane on 28–31 December 1934, England winning by nine wickets.

South Africa and New Zealand have witnessed only one instance apiece of a bowler taking all ten wickets in a first-class innings and both were completed on 28 December. In 1889 A E Moss of Canterbury took 10 for 28 against Wellington to become the only bowler to take all ten wickets in his first first-class match. Seventeen years later A E E (Bert) Vogler of Eastern Province bowled unchanged throughout both innings to take 16 Griqualand West wickets in the day, including 10 for 26 in the second innings.

At Christchurch on 26–27 December 1952, Bert Sutcliffe scored 385 in 461 minutes to establish the current record score in New Zealand first-class cricket. Playing in a Plunket Shield match against Canterbury, he scored his runs out of an Otago total of 500 which proved sufficient for an innings victory.

Glenn Turner, the last player to score a thousand runs before June and a triple century in a single day, made his first-class debut for Otago on Christmas Day 1964 whilst he was still attending school in Dunedin, New Zealand.

Bill Frindall

Tennis at Christmas

O n the northern hemisphere one does not normally think of tennis as a Christmas activity. The ambience of the sport is the summer, despite indoor courts. On the vicarage lawns of England, where the game began, and on the turf of the cricket and baseball clubs in New England in the US, where the game took root as well, it was a summer sport from the start.

Yet it is clear that the man who 'invented' lawn tennis, the immortal Major Walter Clopton Wingfield, visualised his game being played in the depths of the winter.

In his famous pamphlet, which he issued in February, 1874 to publicise his *Sphairistike*, and of which only a handful of copies are known to survive of the first edition, he specifically mentions only one surface on which it might be played. And that surface, incredibly, was ice! And with the players wearing skates! How much more Christmasy can you get?

The whole tone of the booklet is wintry. In the first place W C W (as Wingfield identifies himself) dedicates it on the title page to 'The Party Assembled at Nantclwyd, December 1873'. Nantclwyd is in the depths of North Wales, no place for sport in the sun at that time.

It is clear that the worthy major, formerly of the King's Dragoon Guards and then one of the officers of Her Majesty's Body-guard of Gentlemen-at-Arms, and whose efforts inspired the growth of the world's most widely played sport after soccer, had a Christmas activity in mind.

Major Walter Clopton Wingfield

His introduction reads:

The game of tennis may be traced back to the days of the ancient Greeks, under the name of *Sphairistike*. It was subsequently played by the Romans under the name of *Pila*. It was the fashionable pastime of the nobles of France during the reign of Charles V, and it was in vogue in England as early as Henry III and is described by Gregory as 'one of the most ancient games in Christendom'. Henry V, Henry VII and Henry VIII were all tennis players and it has only now died out owing to the difficulties of the game and the expense of erecting courts. All these difficulties have now been surmounted by the inventor of 'Lawn Tennis', which has all the interest of tennis and has the advantage that it may be played in the open air in any weather by people of any age and of both sexes. In a hard frost the nets may be erected on the ice and, the players being equipped with skates, the game assumes a new feature and gives an opening for the exhibition of much grace and science'.

Thus Major Wingfield. Whoever, one may wonder, has seen the 'grace and science' of tennis on ice!

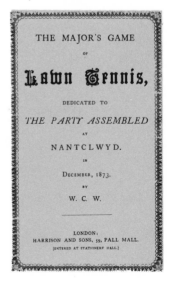

THE MAJOR'S GAME

OF

Lawn Tennis,

DEDICATED TO

THE PARTY ASSEMBLED

AT

NANTCLWYD.

IN

DECEMBER, 1873.

BY

W. C. W.

LONDON:
HARRISON AND SONS, 59, PALL MALL.
[ENTERED AT STATIONERS' HALL.]

BILL BOWREY

Another champion born on Christmas Day was Bill Bowrey, born in Sydney on 25 December, 1943. He was men's singles champion of Australia in 1968. He played for Australia in the Davis Cup in 1968 and 1969.

He had the distinction of being the men's singles winner of the British Under 21 Championships when they were held for the first time in Manchester in 1962. They were last staged in 1980.

In 1968 he married the Australian international Lesley Turner, for years second only to the great Margaret Court.

The Toughest Christmas Match

For twenty-three years after the Second World War the Challenge Round of the Davis Cup (replaced by a Final Round in 1972) saw Australia as one of the participants. The USA were their opponents on the first fourteen of these dramatic occasions.

Australia staged the climax tie in 1946, 1951, 1952, 1953, 1954, 1956, 1957, 1958, 1960, 1961, 1962, 1963, 1965, 1966, 1967, 1968 and 1977. On most occasions it was essentially a Christmas affair. The ties, each comprising two singles on the first day, a doubles on the second with the reverse singles on the third, began on Boxing Day. At no time in Australian history was competitive tennis staged on Christmas Day itself. None the less, the timing of the matches put an end to all hopes of normal Christmas festivities by the teams. It was training, hard and rigorous.

The toughness of the tennis may usefully be measured by the total number of games played. The 1958 Challenge Round tie in Brisbane in which the US beat Australia 3–2 was the longest tie ever staged in the Challenge or Final Round. The total number of games for the five rubbers was 270.

In the opening singles Alex Olmedo (Peruvian-born but playing for the US) beat Mal Anderson 8–6 2–6 9–7 8–6. Then Ashley Cooper, for Australia, levelled the scores by beating Barry MacKay 4–6 6–3 6–2 6–4. That was 89 games for Boxing Day.

In the doubles the Americans took the lead again. Olmedo and Ham Richardson (a rare figure in the game in being both a

FRANKIE DURR, CHRISTMAS DAY CHAMPION

The most notable tennis champion to be born on Christmas Day was Françoise Durr, the greatest French player of the post-Second World War period.

She was born in Algiers on Christmas Day, 1942. She won the women's singles championship of France at the Stade Roland Garros in Paris in 1967.

She won the women's doubles five times, the mixed three. She was Wimbledon mixed doubles champion with the Australian Tony Roche in 1976.

Her style owed nothing to the textbooks. Her backhand was unique. It was said of her that she not only played her backhand from the wrong foot but she often played it from the wrong knee! She married an American, Boyd Browning, in 1975.

Rhodes Scholar and a diabetic) beat Anderson and Neale Fraser 10–12 3–6 16–14 6–3 7–5. This mammoth contest added 82 more games, making 171 for the two days.

The third day of Christmas saw America make victory certain when Olmedo beat Cooper 6–3 4–6 6–4 8–6. In the fifth rubber Anderson beat MacKay 7–5 13–11 11–9. That was 99 more games, making 270 in all.

The toughest Boxing Day belonged to the year before, 1957. The US were the opponents and the setting the Kooyong courts in Melbourne. The Australians took a lead of 2–nil (and eventually 3–nil before a final 3–2 victory). Ashley Cooper beat Vic Seixas 3–6 7–5 6–1 1–6 6–3. That was 44 games. Mal Anderson then beat Barry MacKay 6–3 7–5 3–6 7–9 6–3. That was 55 more and day's total of 99 games, a Boxing day record.

Individually the greatest Boxing Day hardship was experienced by Fred Stolle of Australia and Manuel Santana in the Challenge Round of 1965. It was Spain's first appearance at that stage and they were very much the underdogs.

Even so the Spanish Santana excelled himself in the opening singles. Stolle was thankful to climb back from the loss of the first two sets to win 10–12 3–6 6–1 6–4 7–5.

60 games for the one singles. It was a memorable Christmas for both!

Lance Tingay

VIII

Anniversaries

Famous People Born on Christmas Day

Sir Isaac Newton

1642

Sir Isaac Newton – English mathematician and physicist. Famous for his discoveries in the fields of gravitation, planetary motion and optics. One of the developers of differential and integral calculus. Best known works – *Philosophiae Naturalis Principia Mathematica* (1687) and *Opticks* (1704). Died in 1727.

1716

Johann Jakob Reiske – Born in Zörbig, Saxony (now GDR). Expert on Arabic and Greek literature who laid foundation for future Arabic historical scholarship. Best known work – *Abulfedae Annales Moslemici* (1754). Died in 1774.

1721

William Collins – Born in Chichester, Sussex, he was one of the finest English lyric poets. Best known work – *Persian Eclogues*. He suffered from mental illness from 1751 to his death in 1759.

1759

Richard Porson – Norfolk-born classical Greek scholar. Professor of Greek at Trinity College, Cambridge. Edited plays of Aeschylus and Euripides. Often a boor and a drunkard, he was nevertheless admired for his learning and wit. Died in 1808.

1771

Dorothy Wordsworth – Much loved sister and housekeeper to the poet William. Born in Cockermouth, Cumberland, her own writings, *Alfoxen Journal 1798* and *Grasmere Journals 1800–03*, both published after her death, record the most important creative years of her brother's life. Died in 1855.

1821

Clara Barton – Founded the American Red Cross in 1881 and was its President for 23 years. Originally a schoolteacher, and then a government clerk, she organised relief for the wounded in the American Civil War. Afterwards at President Lincoln's request she set up a bureau to locate missing soldiers. Died in 1912.

1871

Aleksandr Nikolayevich Scriabin – Russian composer and virtuoso pianist. Dabbled in mysticism and used his own harmonic chord. Mainly known for his piano compositions, especially ten sonatas and a concerto. Died in 1915.

1876

Mohamed Ali Jinnah – Indian Muslim politician who founded the state of Pakistan in 1947. Originally studied law, in Britain. Entered politics in 1906. As the first Governor-General of the new state he was its first leader. Died in 1948.

1883

Maurice Utrillo – French painter, particu-

OLYMPIC CHAMPIONS BORN ON CHRISTMAS DAY

1884	Samuel Berger (USA) – won 1904 heavyweight boxing title
1891	Klas Särner (Sweden) – member of 1920 gold medal gymnastics team
1897	Noël Delberghe (France) – member of 1924 gold medal water polo team
1899	Noel Purcell (GB) – member of 1920 gold medal water polo team
1910	Thomas Webster (USA) – 1932 8m class yachting
1925	Rosa 'Ossi' Reichert (Germany) – 1956 slalom skiing champion
1937	Oleg Grigoryev (USSR) – 1960 bantamweight boxing champion

1949   István Osztrics
(Hungary) –
member of 1972
gold medal épée
team

OTHER SPORT

1933   Basil Heatley (GB)
– world record
for 10 miles in
1961.

larly renowned for his pictures of Montmartre street scenes. Took up painting as therapy for alcoholism. Died in 1955.

1885

Paul Manship – American sculptor. His best known works include *Dancer and Gazelles* (1916), the *Prometheus Fountain* in the Rockefeller Center Plaza, New York (1934), and the *Paul Rainey Memorial Gateway* at the Bronx Zoo (1934). Died in 1966.

1887

Conrad Hilton – American hotel magnate. Starting with an inn opened by his father, he eventually headed the world's largest hotel chain, with over 125 hotels throughout the world. Died in 1979.

1892

Dame Rebecca West – Irish-born journalist, novelist and critic. Real name Cicely Isabel Fairfield. Originally trained to be an actress. Author of numerous novels and other books, she received great acclaim for her reporting of the Nuremberg war crimes trials after the Second World War.

1892

Sir Noël Vansittart Bowater – businessman elected Lord Mayor of London 1953–4.

1899

Humphrey Bogart – American film actor, usually playing tough crooks or detectives. Best known films include *The Maltese Falcon* (1941), *Casablanca* (1942), and *The*

African Queen (1952), for which he received the Academy Award. Died in 1957.

1901

Princess Alice, Duchess of Gloucester – third daughter of the Duke of Buccleuch, she married HRH the Duke of Gloucester in 1935 and had two sons.

1905

Baron Westwood – William Westwood succeeded his father in 1953. Vice-President of the Football Association 1974–81. Honorary Vice-President from 1981.

Humphrey Bogart

1906

Baron Grade – Lew Grade was created a life peer in 1976, having been knighted in 1969. Chairman and Chief Executive of ATV Network Limited. Businessman and entertainment industry mogul.

1907

Andrew Cruikshank – Scottish-born stage, screen and radio actor. Best known for his characterisation of Dr Cameron in the TV series *Dr Finlay's Casebook*.

1907

Cab Calloway – American black bandleader and singer. Made a number of films, his first being *The Big Broadcast* in 1932.

1911

Sir Charles Mott-Radclyffe – Member of Parliament for Windsor 1942–70. Parlia-

Mohamed Anwar Sadat

mentary Private Secretary to the Secretary of State for India 1944–5.

1916

Baron Annan – Noël Gilroy Annan created life peer in 1965. Multi-faceted public career.

1918

Mohamed Anwar Sadat – Army officer who became Vice-President of Egypt under his friend Gamal Abdel Nasser, and then succeeded him as President in October, 1970. Awarded the Nobel Peace Prize (with Israel's Menachem Begin) in 1978. Assassinated in 1981.

1936

Princess Alexandra – the Hon Mrs Angus Ogilvy (married in April 1963), one son and one daughter. Daughter of the Duke of Kent and Princess Marina of Greece.

1945

Alice Cooper – real name Vincent Furnier. Outrageous pop music singer. Headed the best selling records list in July, 1972, with *School's Out*.

Famous People Who Died on Christmas Day

62

Persius (Aulus Persius Flaccus) – Wealthy Roman Stoic poet who wrote a celebrated book of six *Satires*, published after his death. Born in 34.

1676

Sir Matthew Hale – Chief Justice of the King's Bench 1671–6. Expert on the history of English Common Law. Member of Parliament for Oxford. Born in 1609.

1712

William King – English poet and wit. Born in 1663.

1875

Thomas Morris – 'Young' Tom was the youngest player ever to win the Open golf championship, aged 17 years 249 days in 1868. Never recovered from the accidental death of his wife and baby 3 months previously. Born in 1851.

1935

Paul Borget – French poet, novelist and critic. Works include *Cruelle Eñigme* (1885), *Le Disciple* (1889), and *Un Divorce* (1904). Born 1852.

1938

Karel Capek – Internationally famous novelist and playwright, who began his career as a journalist. The name he gave to the human-looking machine in his play *R.U.R.* (1920) provided the world with a new word – robot. Born in Bohemia in 1890.

1946

W C Fields – born William Claude Duken-

W C Fields

field in 1880. American film comedian best known for his cynical wit. Usually played character of a heavy drinking, child-and-dog-hating, confidence man. Highly acclaimed portrayal of Mr Micawber in *David Copperfield* (1935).

1961

Otto Loewi – German-born physician and pharmacologist. Awarded Nobel Prize (with Sir Henry Dale) for Physiology of Medicine in 1936, for discoveries relating to the chemical transmission of nerve impulses. Born in 1873.

1977

Charles Spencer Chaplin – multi-talented film star, born in London in 1889. Remembered for his 'little tramp' character in silent films. He also wrote screenplays and directed and composed incidental music for his films. Best known works include *The Gold Rush* (1925), *Modern Times* (1936), and *The Great Dictator* (1940).

Stan Greenberg

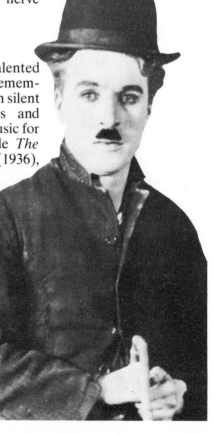